INSPIRATIONAL STORY-TELLING REFLECTIONS
Discovering God in the Everyday

DEVOTIONS
JOURNEY INTO GOD

BY

BARRY BOYTON

(and friends)

Published by
Verbum Publications

Verbum
Publications

ISBN:
978-0-9929573-8-4

First edition published 2022

Printed in the UK

* * * * *

Cover Design by Designed4Print
Cover photo: West Bay, Dorset, taken by the Author

DEDICATION

To
Marion my wife,
and
Anna and Chloe our two dear daughters

These three individuals whom I love deeply are the centre of my world.

I also dedicate this book to the 'Friends of Oddments' many of whom I hardly know, who have been kind enough to support myself and 'Oddments Theatre' financially and in prayer over the years. Without your help I wouldn't have had the privilege to be able to write plays and books and travel the country performing theatre. So 'Thank you - You made it possible'.

CONTENTS

ACKNOWLEDGEMENTS

No book is completed without the help, contribution, and encouragement of others.

This, my second book, is very different from my first one, a story-telling theatre sketch book entitled *Fish and Chips*. That being so, I have needed to take an entirely different approach with this book. I have had many contributors giving their time and attention over several months – years even, and I am truly grateful to all that have helped bring this book to fruition.

I am indebted to Emma Handcock and Joanna Hodgson, my right-hand people over the years. We travelled many miles, performed endless shows, and shared laughs and a few tears together. You always went the extra mile because you cared. Thank you.

Also, Jenny Costigan, who quietly worked behind the scenes keeping us afloat.

And of course, my wife, (my rock), for your endless help and support.

Page contributions from:
Marion Boyton, Joanna Hodgson, Joe Hardy, Steve Legg, Sarah Horder, Peter Idris Taylor, Keith Glover, Julian Lukins, Matt Neil.

Being dyslexic I had help with proof reading and editing from:
Racheal Anderson, Roger Allen, Marion Boyton, Lisa Collins, Anna Chilvers, Ellie Goodall, Emma Handcock, Di Pavey, Matt Lee, Karen Hibbert, Ian Miles, Stephanie Wolf, Dani Taylor, Sadie Dryer, Fiona Green and Alex Parsons.

And special thanks go to:
Doctor Ronald Clements and Tom Goymour who painstakingly edited and formatted the book.

You are all Heroes

FOREWORD

Barry Boyton, founder of Oddments Theatre Company and author of the Christian sketch book *Fish & Chips,* shares a series of devotions through the medium of storytelling. This book contains a combination of insightful reflections to guide & help you in your own quiet times with God.

Having worked with Barry for many years, I can see how his creativity and theatre experience has influenced his writing. He's a natural storyteller and loves to connect with people through their life stories. Barry has a strong faith and a desire to see peoples lives changed through the work of the Holy Spirit. This has been his central motivation in all projects since I've known him an reading the devotions in this book assures me this time is no different.

Based on prominent figures of the Christian faith and personal experiences, I found that these stories from past and present inspired me in my own faith. They've also challenged me to step out of my comfort zone, learning to rely on God and trust in His calling in all areas of my life. When life becomes hard it can be easy to either turn inwards and shut everyone out, or to turn your frustrations out on the world. But through this book, with its strong biblical and historical foundation, Barry helps us to turn our heads and our hearts towards Christ.

I hope you find this book a blessing and an encouragement in your own walk with God as I have.

Emma Handcock

AUTHOR'S PREFACE

I like to entertain and tell a story. That's why I run a theatre company and have the privilege of spending time on stage acting and touring. There is no better story to tell than man's relationship with God. The Bible reveals God through both the Old Testament and later through the central character of Jesus in the New Testament.

My aim of writing this devotions book was to produce a book that is enjoyable to read, contains a lot of variety and is both educational, and thought provoking. I have deliberately ordered this book so that it rarely appears to have any obvious continuity from theme to theme. This is to ensure that the wide range of topics throughout the book give you the expectation that every page turned will be like a new scene of a play for you to enjoy. Basically, I have written a book that I would want to read and enjoy myself. I hope the different themes will inspire, encourage, and deepen your journey into God.

I wondered, 'What qualifies someone to write a book of devotions such as this? Do you have to have a certain level of holiness or spiritual knowledge to bring the hope of Jesus to people? Do you require a certain level of education?' If you need the above qualifications, I am not a good candidate; firstly, I am hugely dyslexic and cannot spell for anything, putting pen to paper takes me twice as long as the average person. Then secondly, of course, I am all too aware of my own sins and failings; the moments when I find little patience or kindness or compassion. I don't have a degree in English literature or theology, so I don't qualify in terms of the academic grey matter either. I am not wise or well educated by human standards.

However, having a living faith in Jesus, changes everything.

1 Corinthians 1: 26-28 NIV Says:

"Think of what you were when you were called. Not many of you were wise by human standards; not many were influential; not many were of noble birth.

But God chose the foolish things of the world to shame the wise; God chose the weak things of the world to shame the strong. God chose the lowly things of this world and the despised things—and the things that are not—to nullify the things that are."

Following Christ changed my life and my career. I started a part time Christian theatre company *(Oddments Theatre Co.)* which developed into a full-time ministry, touring productions with a Christian message to churches, schools, and prisons around the United Kingdom. I particularly like working in prisons and chatting to men whose lives have been transformed by discovering the Christian faith.

This devotional book took me over five years to research and write. Sometimes it was a painfully slow struggle, at other times it was as if God was using my fingers to type the message. I have included devotions I call 'life lessons', gained from experience of touring and leadership. I've met many people whose sacrificial living is truly impressive and it points me to God. I have also met believers with an 'attitude', others stuck in legalism, and people whose core motivation is self-interest, and their agenda quite alarming!

The good news though, is that most of the people I have encountered are inherently good and generous, and their spirit is clearly filled with a deep love for God. These are people who are a walking example of the Christian faith.

I hope this book will encourage you in your journey into God through whatever stage of that journey you are at. I pray that the Holy Spirit will lift the appropriate words and passages from the text and embed them in your heart, so that at times of discouragement there will be stories of hope.

Enjoy, be encouraged, be inspired and find a deeper foundation in Christ.

Barry Boyton

DEVOTIONS
THE JOURNEY BEGINS ...

A Bad Day Good

"The one who gets wisdom loves life; the one who cherishes understanding will soon prosper"

(Proverbs 19:8 NIV).

At a Christian exhibition, an organisation that promoted child sponsorship had a full-sized inflatable elephant as centrepiece on their stand. The enormity of it took up so much of the stand's space that it gave the promotional staff little room to work. But it achieved its aim of attracting attention. Printed across the plastic body of the elephant was the question: 'How do you eat an elephant?'

The whole thing seemed a little out of sentiment with Christian concerns about caring for God's creation, but the idea behind the campaign was to get you to ask the question, 'How do you eat an elephant?' Like many before me, I felt compelled to ask this question. The answer: 'One bit at a time.'

The organisation then linked the answer to how we can reduce child poverty one child at a time and how sponsorship would help. Personally, I disliked the idea of linking eating an elephant to sponsoring a child in need, but the question is a good one. How do you achieve something? The description of the task is pinpoint accurate: 'one bit at a time'.

Each of us, at some stage, will feel overwhelmed: challenges from work, family pressures, deadlines to meet, bills to pay and emails to respond too. These are all things that demand our time and emotional energy to resolve.

It is easy to experience a feeling of helplessness as if you are defeated before you start, but by simply tackling one thing at a time you can overcome this. The real challenge however is to know what to prioritise. That is where wisdom is needed. Maybe, if there is a lesson to learn from the large inflatable elephant, it is that not everything has to be done today. Wisdom releases us from the crushing pressures of obligation and shows us the joy of life that can turn a bad day good.

Prayer:
Lord, help me to know the right path to take. Help me to ignore what is unnecessary, distracting and unfruitful. I ask you to implant in me your wisdom that helps me to discern what is right and lay aside what is not.
Amen.

A Child's Inheritance

"Children are a heritage from the Lord, offspring a reward from him"

(Psalm 127:3 NIV).

Inheritance is so often associated with money, the passing on of stored wealth to the next generation in the hope it will make a difference. I believe a real child's inheritance is more than a gift of money. It is the things money cannot buy that are of the greatest value. The gift of love and time are priceless in a child's life. As a parent, it is this unconditional love that only you can give, a currency beyond pounds or dollars. Creating time for your offspring is the greatest investment you ever make. I believe each day of our lives we can make deposits in the memory banks of our children, helping them to build a foundation for the future. I love what Proverbs 22: 6 (NIV) says 'Start children off on the way they should go, and even when they are old they will not turn from it'.

I heard it said, 'If you want to have your children turn out well, don't turn your home into a lunch counter and lodging house', be there for them. The best inheritance a parent can leave their children is a few minutes of their time each day. Don't be a parent who misses out on your child's childhood because of work demands or any personal ambitions or over commitment. Work will always have its demands, friends will come and go, but children are an inheritance from the Lord. Let's not sacrifice our children's spiritually and emotional inheritance because we are just too busy. It is better to live in a home full of love than a house full of gadgets and possessions. You can never buy back the time you didn't invest in your children. The inheritance you leave should be one of love, not money.

Prayer:
Lord help me to be a good parent, show me how to love and care. In my moments of weakness and discouragement, when my parenting didn't go well, help me to realise a bad day doesn't define a lifetime of parenting. Help me be an example of kindness and love over the coming years.

Amen.

A Difficult Conversation – Sex

"Do not deprive each other except perhaps by mutual consent and for a time, so that you may devote yourselves to prayer"

(1 Corinthians 7:5 NIV).

I used to run my own little electrical installation company rewiring people's homes. One of my customers, a school mistress, much older than myself who devoted years to ministering in the Salvation Army, asked me to upgrade a few circuits. As the work ran over a few days, we developed a nice habit of having tea breaks during which we chatted. At 3.00 pm. a cup of tea would be served in the living room where we would converse and half watch the television, which would always be switched on.

One day, a chat show programme was being broadcast and the presenter suddenly announced, 'Now we have a couple joining us who want to recycle your vibrators and sex toys.' Then the couple started to show various models of sex toys designed to bring excitement to people's sex lives. We both sat there in silence watching the screen while they demonstrated some of the buzzing devices and odd shaped toys. They were encouraging people to use their company to recycle them for others to use. Twenty minutes passed and the article concluded. Then it was back to work without either of us uttering a single word of acknowledgement of what we had seen. It was as though those moments were erased from time. Of course, I wouldn't have wanted an in-depth conversation about the programme's contents, but maybe we should at least have acknowledged it happened rather than simply sweeping it under the carpet?

The problem of continually sweeping awkward or difficult subjects under the carpet is that eventually the pile gets bigger until someone trips over it. Some subjects are sensitive to talk about as they expose our own fears and vulnerabilities. Whether you are married or single, talking about sex can be an awkward subject. Of course, sex is joked about in general terms, and it helps to sell some newspapers. The problem with light-hearted banter is that it can give the impression everyone is 'at it', having sex a lot more frequently than is actually happening. Moreover, married couples soon discover children can become a great form of contraception. Easily accessed Internet pornography can be a poor substitute for intimacy.

In marriage, we must never forget that physical union is one of the layers of glue that binds the marriage together. Yet, for many, this can be one of the subjects we avoid taking about in depth. To have an honest conversation about sex is necessary, not just for the act of making love but for emotional connection and intimacy. It takes courage and gentleness to start these dialogues. Whatever we do, let's not sweep the subject of sex and intimacy under the carpet. Sex in marriage is whatever you make it, but it may improve with a conversation!

A Fine Line

They say that pride usually causes a fall.
It's a risk that I take when I try to walk tall.

It's such a precipitous fine line to fathom,
a tight rope suspended across a deep chasm.
A dangerous minefield, a difficult challenge,
of stepping out boldly, whilst keeping my balance.

But listening intently to Father's voice,
will help to inform my decisions and choice
Of trust in Him, not self-reliance, of faithfulness not arrogance.
Happy for everyone to see, any gifting I have, is not from me.

In Him I find my security, in Him I find my identity.
With His acceptance, love and truth, there's nothing left for me to prove.
So now, when trying to walk tall, I'm no longer afraid to fall.
A sturdy bridge of love and hope has now replaced the thinnest rope.

Marion Boyton

A Judge's Nightmare

"Then Jesus told his disciples a parable... He said: 'In a certain town there was a judge who neither feared God nor cared what people thought. And there was a widow in that town who kept coming to him with the plea, "Grant me justice against my adversary." For some time he refused. But finally, he said to himself, 'Even though I don't fear God or care what people think, yet because this widow keeps bothering me, I will see that she gets justice, so that she won't eventually come and attack me!'"

(Luke 18: 1-5 NIV).

We see in this parable two characters both initially entrenched in their position. There is 'The Campaigner', she was determined, she had a cause to fight. She was out there lobbying hard to get a just result. In fact, she was one of those people who just doesn't want to get off on the wrong foot. Her ability to press the issue home was unrelenting, she simply never gave up the fight.

Then there is 'The judge' who, I expect, knew she had a case but for whatever reason couldn't be bothered to address her issues. It was not on his priority list. In fact, she was an irritation – like a fly buzzing around a room when one is trying to sleep. Her case was a complete nuisance to him, one he would have liked to have confined to a corner of the office to collect dust.

What I love about this story is the dogged persistence of the woman. I believe there are a couple of points we can take on board.

- No battle is won without a persistent fight

- The Bible passage says, 'So that she won't eventually come and attack me!' There is a warning here to avoid trouble.

I was talking to an employment lawyer who told me that 'if a problem isn't addressed early and solved quickly, the situation can uncontrollably escalate.

Point to ponder: Got a problem? Own it, address it, sort it.

It makes for a far more peaceful life – ask the judge.

Alive and Kicking

A while ago, my wife received a letter from the NHS in which they mentioned the fact that she was a widow. This came as a big surprise to her and an even bigger one to me! It reminded me that I often hear progressive thinkers citing the premature demise of God. They state that the progress of knowledge has finally made it impossible for any thoughtful person to believe in God. Therefore, God is officially dead!

Further fuel was added to this theory in 2018 when a survey found that when people needed deep answers, seventy percent searched Google, whereas less than thirty percent prayed. It doesn't need pointing out that I am not writing this from beyond the grave, but it may come as a surprise to some that God is not dead. During the Covid-19 outbreak, Google noted a huge increase of people searching for information on how to pray! It would seem that when science and our knowledge can't find an answer for those life shattering events like a pandemic, people start to look to God for the answers. Maybe it's because as it has been said, everyone has an inborn sense of deity. This is why anthropologists have never discovered a tribe of atheists.

It would seem that to kill off belief in God, we would need to blot out the stars, turn the orderly process of creation around us into chaos, and perform a lobotomy on every human being! Moreover, we would need to remove from history any trace of the name and life of Jesus! Not the easiest thing to do at Christmas or Easter time. Yet God can be as good as dead to us if we ignore his reaching out through his Son Jesus into our lives. By acting as such, we can treat God as though he didn't exist. In the film *The Jazz Singer*, Neil Diamond's father declares that his son is as good as dead to him; in fact, he declares that he has no son! Diamond wasn't dead, it was just that his father refused to acknowledge him as alive because he was so angry with him. What about you, is God dead or alive to you? Prayer is as easy as talking to a friend. If you don't believe me, google it.

Rev. Keith Glover

Amy Carmichael

(1867–1951)

Amy Carmichael was a missionary and Author who rescued young girls from temple prostitution in India. *(Young girls were given to Hindu temples and the priests would educate them in exchange for their services. In theory, they were given by parents to be married to gods. In reality they were virtual prisoners used by the priests and others who paid for sexual satisfaction. For women there would be no escape).*

Compelled by the love of God Amy opened an orphanage and founded a mission in Dohnavur. She later supported boys in the low caste system. She lived in India for fifty-five years without returning home. She wrote thirty-five books. This is her remarkable story.

The death of Amy's father from pneumonia turned her world upside down as the family then struggled to financially survive. The difficulties led to Amy being withdrawn from her Belfast private school at seventeen, to help raise four of her six siblings.

One day returning from church, she came across a beggar woman in rags from the Belfast slums struggling to carry a heavy bundle of firewood. With her brother's help they saw the old women home and witnessed first-hand the terrible living conditions of the slums. A year later, at the age of eighteen, she volunteered on Saturday evenings to give out food and gospel leaflets in the district. She then decided to move into their rundown neighbourhood and live like one of them; even sleeping in a bug-infested bed. Carmichael got permission to hold gospel meetings at a local church but faced much protest from members who objected to the poor lice-infected visitors taking up all the spaces in their church. Within two years four hundred women and girls were attending. After much prayer, a building plot was miraculously obtained and a church called *The Welcome* was built. It became a haven of God's love and a place of much activity for the area.

A move to England brought about an encounter with Robert Wilson, the cofounder of the Keswick Convention. Amy became his right-hand woman, helping with the demands of hospitality and administration of the home and ministry. She was inspired after hearing Hudson Taylor speak about his missionary work, but Amy was an unlikely candidate as she suffered bouts of poor heath that would often leave her bedridden for weeks on end. Because of her frailty, the China Inland Mission rejected her. Eventually, there was an opportunity to serve in Japan, but due to ill heath she was only able to stay there for fifteen months. But God had other plans for this young woman. In 1895 the Church of England Zenana Mission accepted her to go to southern India.

Arriving in India, she entered a country bustling with life, exotic aromas and colour, but one that had an underlying darker story. The missionary plan was to use a small village called Dohnavur as a temporary base for missionary activity in Southern India.

It was here Amy was to find her life calling when a screaming seven-year-old child jumped into her lap, clinging to her neck. Unbeknown to Amy, the little girl had escaped from a Hindu temple where her mother had given her to the priests in hopes of winning the favour of the gods. There, young girls were groomed, so that at puberty they could become temple prostitutes of the Brahmin priests who gave them no rights. All Amy knew at that moment was that this frightened girl needed her love and protection. Once the horrible facts were established, Amy adopted the little girl, but she was not to be a mother to only one child; as the years rolled by more girls sought sanctuary and she devoted herself to rescuing these youngsters from an otherwise bleak future. Mainly, children arrived on her doorstep, but on other occasions she would travel long distances on hot and dusty roads just to try and save one child. Amy wore a sari and sometimes she coloured her skin with coffee so as to not arouse suspicion of her native ancestry on these daring missions. But her attempts were not always successful. Amy experienced victory and defeat as the work grew. The bondage of the caste system that dominated society was a constant battle.

Over time, the Dohnavur site developed and provided a haven for over one thousand children who might otherwise have died or, at best become sexual fodder or slaves. The growing community of helpers provided physical and spiritual help for all. In 1918, it expanded to include boys. Amy wrote many books, the work became recognised as one of the most successful missionary endeavours of its time, a shining example of love and prayer.

In 1931, Carmichael was badly injured in a fall which left her in constant pain and bedridden for the remainder of her life. She died in India in 1951 at the age of 83.

An Action-packed Read

"Has the Lord as much pleasure in your burnt offerings and sacrifices as in your obedience? Obedience is far better than sacrifice. He is much more interested in your listening to him than in your offering the fat of rams to him"

(1 Samuel 15:22 NIV).

How many words can you fit onto a Hebrew scroll?

Not enough sometimes. In the case of Samuel 1 and 2, rather than two books, it should have been one continuous manuscript, but the scrolls were simply not adequate to fit all the text on. The books of Samuel were completed about 550 BC and are part of Israel's ancient history and focus on the transformation from the Judges to the rule of kings.

Do you love action packed drama?

If so, these two books are for you, They've got it all; storyline, family feuds, leadership rivalry, assassination plots, (1 Sam 11 NIV), multiple wars, and a punch up with a giant, (1 Sam 17 NIV). And for some gruesome action, there is some ethnic cleansing of the Amalekites (1 Sam 15: 1-9 NIV). That's not all, you will encounter the Witch of Endor (1 Sam 28 NIV), discover the idol in bed with goat's hair (1 Sam 19:15 NIV), and even a King who takes his own life (1 Sam 31: 1-13 NIV).

The story is told through three central characters Samuel, Saul and David over a timeline of one hundred years. The book of Samuel is brutally honest, highlighting the political and military achievements of the leading players, (1 Sam 5:1-12 NIV), but exposing their fawned moral failing.

Samuel is a spiritual agent of God, political reformer, King Maker, judge and Priest. He is the person calling for national renewal of faith.

Saul was the first anointed king of Israel but relied on his own judgement and not God's plan. He was a tragically disobedient ruler of Israel, who over time became unstable which led to him taking his own life.

David was God's appointed second king. David was a man after Gods' own heart, but he had a lapse of judgement and let lust get the better of him when saw a beautiful nude Bathsheba. David's adulterous relationship led to the murder of her innocent husband (2 Sam 11:1-24 NIV). However, David found solace in the Lord and God forgave him, this is reflected in songs of praise in Psalm 51. 1-2 (NIV).

These two books may not fit onto one scroll, but historically, they can teach us so much about the human condition and God's ways.

It's an action packed read.

(Suggested Reading: Samuel 1 and 2 NIV)

Angry Children / Despairing Parents

"And he shall turn the heart of the fathers to the children, and the heart of the children to their fathers"

(Malachi 4:5 NIV).

Have you ever felt a failure as a parent? You know your shortcomings, but you've done your best to bring up your children and support them. Yet, sitting at the dining room table, you are faced with an angry teenager who acts like they hate you. Their ability to launch a subtle sarcastic verbal assault still catches you off guard. The blow is painfully wounding and you feel the agony of disappointment. Where did you go wrong? Your dreams that there would be a strong bond between you seem like a notion that is slowly dissipating as the child transforms from the cocoon of childhood to the monster of adolescence.

Many parents are left asking, 'What went wrong? What should I have done?' They blame themselves for failing to make a happy well-balanced teenager that somehow, other parents seem to have managed to have done. Successful parenting isn't an achievement that they are going to add to their CV of life's successes. It's been a struggle to bring up the children, so what is left when morale is drowning under the weight of despair?

It is hope! It may be just a droplet in a bucket full of animosity and rejection, but it's there, a living light faintly shining – a promise of restoration of broken relationships. Malachi 4: 5 (NIV) says: 'He turns the hearts of the fathers to their children and the hearts of the children to their fathers'.

Prayer:
Let us pray for our children in both the good times, and when relationships are strained. For strong family relationships, and restoration of bonds that are fragmented. For my family and my friends' families. Pray where there has been discord that harmony will follow.
Pray that your Holy Spirit will work in the hearts of parents and their offspring and that you Lord will turn the heart of fathers to their children, and the heart of the children to their fathers, and to their mothers'.
Amen.

Any Destination, Any Route, Lots of Possibilities

"For John baptised with water, but in a few days you will be baptised with the Holy Spirit"

(Acts 1:5 NIV).

Have you ever asked yourself how church activity would function without the work of the Holy Spirit? Can I suggest that the majority of church business would carry on uninterrupted. Of course, we could put forward the argument that God gave us the ability to independently make decisions, to plan, organise, and administer. My question is: are we seeking God for advice or are we asking him to bless our already formulated ideas and strategies? In our planning meetings and leadership gatherings, are we really stopping and seeking God and saying, 'Your will be done, Your kingdom come?' Or have we organised everything so well that the Holy Spirit has a seat at the table, but we don't give God time to take his chair before all the discussions have concluded? Church activity shouldn't become like any other association; a functional collection of well-meaning people delivering the objectives of the club or political party for the benefit of the members.

The autobiography of George Müller tells the story of how he established homes for orphaned children in Bristol. I actually found the book rather boring because so many pages are filled with him seeking God. But the more I persevered through the chapters, the more I realised how 'independent' of God I am. George Müller also meditated on the word of God and how to know God's ways.

The challenge for us is not to be good respected people who just administer his work, but people who know the power of God and his ways. We are to be kingdom citizens who have a deep foundation in God's word and a heart open to whatever unexpected journey God may call us upon. We can just choose to fly to any destination and take any route that promises lots of possibilities or hope of success. The problem is that on arrival, we can never truly disembark if the passport of the Holy Spirit has been left behind on the boarding counter.

Prayer:
Holy Spirit, empower me to know the perfect will of God. Thy kingdom come, thy will be done.
Amen.

Are You Sitting Comfortably?

"Designate a place outside the camp where you can go to relieve yourself. As part of your equipment have something to dig with, and when you relieve yourself, dig a hole and cover up your excrement"

(Deuteronomy 23:12-13 NIV).

In the eighteenth century, London was a smelly place to live with woeful sanitation. Cesspits were the norm and were prone to overflow, causing outbreaks of cholera when excrement and urine contaminated the drinking water, resulting in tens of thousands of deaths.

To resolve the cesspit problems the authorities of the day encouraged rainwater gullies to be used to move the human waste directly into the Thames. The river simply became an open sewer. Then the cocktail of the 1858 heatwave combined with the polluted river caused an intoxicating stench known as *The Great Stink.* Politicians found the stench impossible to bear and within eighteen days, the idea put forward by a civil engineer Joseph Bazalgette of an underground sewer system that pumped the waste far from the city was rushed through Parliament. The second great improvement for reducing the sewage smell had already been invented by Alexander Cumming in 1775, it was a flushing toilet designed with an 'S' bend. The design created a water-filled bend and an air tight seal stopping methane gas and other nasty odours wafting back up through the waste pipes. The toilet was demonstrated for the first time in 1851 at the Great exhibition at Crystal Palace. Visitors paid a penny to use it, hence the phrase 'spend a penny'. The roll out of the flushing toilet was slow until Thomas Crapper set himself up as a sanitary engineer, manufacturing toilets at his own brass foundry and workshops. These lavatories and their connected pipes joined the new underground sewage system. Therefore, it moved the human waste away for the capital and reduced the smell. Initially, the waste was dumped raw, further downstream into the Thames, but with the invention of the water treatment works, contaminated waste went through a cleaning process and then was released back into rivers as clean water.

Today we take good sanitation for granted in the western world, yet, one in three people across the world don't have somewhere safe to go to the toilet. Bad sanitation is one of the world's biggest killers. Every 15 seconds a child under the age of five dies because of dirty water and poor sanitation. Around half the people in the world have an illness caused by bad sanitation. In parts of Nairobi, Kenya, some people defecate into a plastic bag and late at night they swing the bag around their head and hurl it as far away as possible – it's called 'the flying toilet', an action that I expect is rather irritating for nearby neighbours, as well as the fact that it spreads disease. In the reading in Deuteronomy 23 it shows God cares about people's toilet habits and safe deposal of waste.

Pray: That leaders of governments around the world will resolve and commit to take action to provide basic sanitation for all people.

Assumptions

"Jesus entered Jericho and was passing through. A man was there by the name of Zacchaeus; he was a chief tax collector and was wealthy. He wanted to see who Jesus was, but because he was short he could not see over the crowd. So he ran ahead and climbed a sycamore-fig tree to see him, since Jesus was coming that way. When Jesus reached the spot, he looked up and said to him, 'Zacchaeus, come down immediately. I must stay at your house today.' So he came down at once and welcomed him gladly. All the people saw this and began to mutter, 'He has gone to be the guest of a sinner.'"

(Luke 19:1-7 NIV).

In Michelle Obama's autobiography, she tells a story of her young children wanting their school friends to come over to play. The White House is no ordinary drop-off point for parents, who firstly had to be security checked to ensure the safety of the presidential family. She noticed that within a very short space of time, once the children had arrived, the kids didn't care about famous residences or surroundings, they just wanted to have fun. On other occasions, she noticed, when she introduced her own young daughters to someone famous that they were totally uninterested and soon zipped off to have fun.

Of course, the way children and adults view the world is completely different. When adults meet someone for the first time, they can unconsciously make assumptions about them, based on their experience, the reputation of the person, what they look like, or the colour of their skin, and all within a few minutes. Interviewing someone for a job, that gentle process of interrogating a person politely can also challenge our bias. I personally have found it hard not to judge the person in front of me, especially if they trigger something that reminds me of another person's characteristics or even their looks, and my reaction can either be positive or negative. Basically, the interview is slightly hoodwinked by the unconscious bias that lurks deep within my being.

I love the story of Zacchaeus, who climbed up a sycamore tree to see Jesus and then Jesus invited himself to his house for tea and biscuits. This act flabbergasted the disciples. 'Don't you know who this man is? What he does? He's a sinner. He's not like us.'

You can imagine the disciples' private thoughts. 'He is not in the exclusive discipleship club.' I wonder why they had such strong prejudices against Zac the tree climber. Were their reactions driven or influenced by prejudice or unconscious bias?

Jesus, on the contrary, looked at the heart not the appearance, and didn't care if Zacchaeus looked rather silly perched on a branch.

I would suggest that each one of us has layers of bias, some unconscious, which affect how we relate to people and how we view the world. We have created invisible barriers of judgement that we have been slowly constructing throughout our life's journey. Each of our assumptions affects our relationships and stops us seeing someone as God sees them.

Question:

Can you identify any bias or assumptions you hold yourself that affect your actions and relationships with others?

Prayer:
Help me Lord not be a person who categorises people into social classes, ethnicity groups, or judges people by gender or sexual bias.
Help me to relate to people with equality. Build me into someone who reacts to others with respect, kindness and friendship.
Lord, help me to have friends of racial diversity, who bring a different perspective to my life.
Amen.

Bashed with Reeds

"And they smote him on the head with a reed, and did spit upon him, and bowing their knees worshipped him"

(Mark 15:19 KJV).

When I envision a reed, I imagine a small bulrush semi-submerged in a river or pond. But in this passage, we are talking about a reed that is more like bamboo. This type of reed may have been Arundo Donax, which grows to the height of three and a half metres and was common in Egypt and Palestine at the time Jesus was there. It is strong and pliable, so in stormy weather its shape temporarily distorts under strong winds but then it returns to its upright position. In this bible passage, I believe that it was used as a rod to inflict suffering upon Jesus. The bamboo-like reed has a cane stem. Maybe this is why the New International Version of the bible translates the word 'reed' as 'staff', They smote him on the head with a reed, unleashing a physical onslaught, the battering he received would have caused severe pain, disorientation and injury. It was in this wounded state that Jesus was mocked and humiliated. The Son of God, who had been assaulted both physically and mentally then had to drag the crushing weight of the cross for his own execution. It was at the cross someone offered Jesus a sponge filled with sour wine on a long reed (bamboo type) to dull the pain 'And one ran and filled a spunge full of vinegar, and put it on a reed, and gave him to drink.'(Mark 15: 36 KJV).

My point is that when we're out and about and we see reeds or bamboo growing in a garden, just like it has done all over the world for centuries, it can remind us of the suffering Christ endured for us – something that is as significant today as it was at the time – just like the bamboo reed!

Blame

"The man said, 'The woman you put here with me – she gave me some fruit from the tree, and I ate it.' Then the Lord God said to the woman, 'What is this you have done?' The woman said, 'The snake deceived me, and I ate'"

(Genesis 3:12-13 NIV).

On 7th May 1915 the passenger liner *Lusitania* was torpedoed by a German U-boat off the Irish coast on its journey from New York to Liverpool. The official figure of people that drowned was 1,198. Within days people were looking for someone to blame for the loss of life. An enquiry followed and the ship's captain, William Turner, was questioned and it was soon implied that he was to blame for the disaster. The facts emerged that the captain was advised to sail in a zig-zag manner to confuse the U-boat but he did not follow this advice! The captain became the target for an ensuing storm of public rage.

Later it emerged that by wholly blaming the captain it had allowed British intelligence to avoided scrutiny from their own failings. The intelligence service knew of the danger but failed to give the vessel any Royal Navy protection. The captain, while partly responsible, was made a scapegoat.

From childhood, blame seems to be a habit we learn. Siblings quickly blame sisters/brothers for something that got broken. This pattern of blaming others and not taking responsibility can continue into adulthood. Husbands and wives blame each other if things go wrong. Criminals blame someone else for grassing them up.

Blame is about not taking responsibility for our actions; it is a smokescreen to hide the truth of our own failings. In today's passage I wonder what would have happened if Eve had said,

'*It's my fault, I decided to take the Fruit.*'

Or Adam had said,

'*I chose to take the fruit and eat from it. It was my decision.*'
But that's not what happened. Both refused to own their responsibility.

Is there a situation where we have moved the blame for our actions onto someone else? Where we should take responsibility for our actions?

Blown Apart

"Be merciful to me, my God, for my enemies are in hot pursuit; all day long they press their attack. My adversaries pursue me all day long; in their pride many are attacking me. When I am afraid, I put my trust in you. In God, whose word I praise – in God I trust and am not afraid. What can mere mortals do to me? All day long they twist my words; all their schemes are for my ruin. They conspire, they lurk, they watch my steps, hoping to take my life."

(Psalm 56: 1-6 NIV).

This Psalm was written when David was in a bad place. He was on the run from King Saul and for some reason was now in the Philistine city of Gath. This city was the home of Goliath, whom he had slain. You can imagine, he was not Mr Popular at the base camp. I suspect that a few diehard fans of Goliath would have been rather keen to revenge the death of their hero. David had made a rod for his own back with enemies in both Israel and Palestine.

The good he did in the past, saving Israel from the Philistine army when he had slain Goliath, then obtaining the position of personal harp player to King Saul, now counted for nothing. All his achievements and the reward of his position changed when Saul took a personal dislike to him and wanted him dead. David must have wondered why this was happening; surely, if you do good in the world, good will follow. This now seemed not to be the case. There are moments in David's story that seem similar to Job's terrible troubles, (Job 1: 6-22 NIV) Another man crashes from great heights to the depths of despair.

I have seen friends who served God faithfully, good people, yet their world was blown apart by an unfortunate change of circumstance. A diagnosis of a terminal illness, being scammed into giving their life savings away, or the loss of a loved one.

We all face circumstances that cause us pain and a sense of disorientation and disappointment. Generally, we learn to adapt and readjust our balance. But what happens when a crushing event leaves a person so mortified that all courage and hope is in tatters. Their world is now blitzed into a wasteland of desolation; an unrecognisable landscape where once supportive friends have retreated to the trenches because they don't know how to react. What does a person do, when completely lost and alone, and fear is the overwhelming emotion?

David faced an impossible situation, but when he was afraid, he put his trust in the Lord.

Prayer :
For those in desperation, struggling with abyss of hopelessness.
Lord have mercy.

For my own battles, in moments of self-doubt and lack of faith.
Lord be my guide.

In times of despair and disorientation.
Lord be my compass.

In times of abundance and of hardship.
Lord be my rock.

For the glory of God
Amen.

Boldness

"Joseph of Arimathea, a prominent member of the Council, who was himself waiting for the kingdom of God, went boldly to Pilate and asked for Jesus' body. Pilate was surprised to hear that he was already dead. Summoning the centurion, he asked him if Jesus had already died. When he learned from the centurion that it was so, he gave the body to Joseph. So Joseph bought some linen cloth, took down the body, wrapped it in the linen, and placed it in a tomb cut out of rock. Then he rolled a stone against the entrance of the tomb"

(Mark 15:43-46 NIV).

In this passage we meet Joseph of Arimathea, a wealthy man and a member of the Sanhedrin council. The great Sanhedrin council were the Jewish supreme court of the day on religious and political affairs. It was the Sanhedrin council that asked Pilate to sentence Jesus to death. However, Joseph of Arimathea had opposed the crucifixion of Jesus (Luke 23: 50-51 NIV). After Jesus' crucifixion, Joseph approached Pontius Pilate and asked him if he could bury the body of Jesus.

A crucified body was state property and the Roman Governor of the province had the power to decide whether to release the body or not. Executed criminals were usually left on the cross in clear view of the public, to discourage similar crimes. Their bodies would be devoured by birds and dogs and when only bones were left, they were tossed into places such as Golgotha (place of Skulls).

Joseph of Arimathea was a Godly person who was waiting for the Messiah. Joseph had pre-planned his own funeral arrangements. His burial plot in accordance with Jewish tradition was situated outside the city wall near Golgotha, a stone's throw from where Jesus was crucified.

It is believed that Joseph was a secret admirer of Jesus. After Christ's death it was Joseph of Arimathea who stepped out of the shadows and took the risk by approaching Pilate; thus, gaining permission to care for the body of Jesus. Then he gave the body of Jesus a proper burial according to Jewish tradition rather than allowing it to be thrown into the unmarked grave of a common criminal. This pinnacle moment is recorded in all four gospels.

I believe Joseph of Arimathea's contribution to history can teach us all an important lesson. His intervention made a difference.

Just like Joseph of Arimathea, our own moments of intervention can make a difference, either short or longer term. Your intervention could change things for just one person or help towards global change over a specific issue – you never know. Our actions become part of history.

Brick to Slick
(The Mobile Phone)

"Do not conform to the pattern of this world, but be transformed by the renewing of your mind. Then you will be able to test and approve what God's will is – his good, pleasing and perfect will"

(Romans 12:2 NIV).

When the mobile phone made its first public appearance in the early 1980s, it was a funny looking device. More like a car battery with a corded telephone attached. This 8lb invention gave the user ample chance to tone their arm muscles alongside making the calls. First carted around by businessmen as a statement of self-importance, the mobile has now evolved into an indispensable possession for over 85% of the world's population. Since the launch of the iPhone in 2007, the world hasn't looked back. From banking to Bible reading, the world really is at our fingertips. A teenager once asked, 'Before mobile phones were invented, how did you watch Netflix?'

The mobile has revolutionised our world. Most would agree it is a fantastic invention, but are the hours we spend on it each day helping us in our walk with the Lord? Are we spending as much time listening to God as we are the people on our social media accounts? Who or what are we allowing to transform our minds? If it's not Jesus, then it's something else. We should acknowledge this and limit the time we spend using our phones and devices.

Prayer:
Dear Father, thank you for the invention of the mobile phone and all the good things we can enjoy from it. Please show us where we conform too much to the pattern of this world and where we need to make changes, so that we can put you first in every area of our lives. Whether it's using Bible reading and prayer apps or turning our phones off completely to focus on you, please help us to live in a way that always puts your good, pleasing and perfect will first.
Amen.

By My Power, Fear Not

'Do not fear, for I have redeemed you; I have summoned you by name; you are mine. When you pass through the waters, I will be with you; and when you pass through the rivers, they will not sweep over you. When you walk through the fire, you will not be burned; the flames will not set you ablaze. For I am the Lord your God, the Holy One of Israel, your Saviour.

(Isaiah 43: 1-3 NIV).

In today's reading, the Babylonians had destroyed Jerusalem in 586 BC after a siege that had lasted nearly two years. The inhabitants were taken into exile to Babylon. We now witness God's plan of deliverance to end years of servitude and captivity. Isaiah encourages them to have no fear, for God will be with them. God will redeem his people from the bondage of living in a foreign land. He will restore them to their homeland. Yahweh will be the one who will walk the difficult journey with them. The promised journey home would not be without danger or void of difficulties. The Israelites may well be afraid, if not overwhelmed. God said 'Don't Fear, for I have redeemed you'.

In our lives, I wonder how many times fear has held us back: the fear of failure, the fear of being rejected, the fear of looking stupid, fear of the unknown, fear of changing jobs. Fears and anxieties can hold us back from becoming the person God wants us to be. When we fail, the experience can have a habit of undermining our confidence, it is an ingrained reaction that disables us before we start. Like the people of Judah in captivity, God is calling us to a time of moving forward and restoration. Journeys can be difficult and sometimes you need help through the valley and up and down the mountains. God is the one who says, 'Do not fear. I have redeemed you.' We just need to take the first step out of fear.

Prayer:
Lord, I know there are areas where I fear, where I lack confidence, where I wish I could be different from who I am. Lord, help me to be the person you want me to be, help me not to be held back by fear. Help me to take a step of faith into your promises.

Amen.

By The Rivers of Babylon

"By the rivers of Babylon we sat and wept when we remembered Zion. There on the poplars we hung our harps, for there our captors asked us for songs, our tormentors demanded songs of joy; they said, 'Sing us one of the songs of Zion!' How can we sing the songs of the Lord while in a foreign land?"

(Psalm 137:1-4 NIV).

The Jewish stronghold of Jerusalem had fallen and its dwellings now lay ransacked by the Babylonian army. The fortified citadel city, which had been besieged for two years by King Nebuchadnezzar, had finally succumbed and fallen when its inhabitants were at the point of starvation. The holy temple was a burned and stripped of its gold, silver and bronze. The once God-fearing nation was swallowed and absorbed into the great all-conquering Babylonian empire. The people were taken into captivity. But while they had lost their motherland, they had not lost their nationality. They still remembered Zion.

This psalm, a communal lamentation, a hymn pouring out deep heart-felt misery, reflected for the Jews a yearning for their homeland while in captivity in a foreign land. Once again, God's people, like the time in Egypt, had their self-determination stripped away and now lived under a yoke of oppression, mockery and a ruthless foreign dictator. Once, the Levites sang inspiring songs in God's temple and it was said that their worship could be heard for miles by those approaching the Holy City. But now, in these days of exile, their joy had turned to mourning. Such was the brokenness of the spirit, they had no motivation to play their harps, so they laid them aside. How could they recreate the music of their Zion temple, while denied the autonomy of their own sovereignty? Why respond to the demands of their oppressors and use their harps, the national instrument of the Hebrews, to entertain? They had not disposed of their instruments but could not bear to play them either. So, there beside the River Euphrates, they hung their harps on poplar trees, maybe this was a silent symbolic statement of deep-rooted grieving.

For many of us the course of life will bring troubled waters; times when the flow of circumstances threatens to drown us; times when we feel God has abandoned us. Times when to worship God seems an alien thing to do – like the Jews in this psalm, their spirits were crushed and despairing. However, the musicians hadn't destroyed their harps as a final violent act of defeatism, they held onto them as a symbol of hope and restoration, but, at that moment in time, their wailing song reflected their trauma. 'How can we sing the songs of the Lord while in a foreign land?' They held onto a faint hope that one day their song of grief would be replaced by one of celebration.

In this psalm there is a lesson for us. Whatever the circumstances, however weak we feel, estranged from love, we must not pack away our faith into the cupboard of despair. Because one day our current song, a lamentation of despair could be replaced by a song of celebration.

Character

"Do not be misled: 'Bad company corrupts good character."

(1 Corinthians 15:33 NIV).

Over the years, I've run many great ministry theatre teams. However, there was one team I remember for all the wrong reasons. On paper, this group of actors was oozing with artistic talent. In the beginning, everything seemed to go well. Everywhere they went, people commented on our first-class team. Then, cracks started to appear; self-motivation traits and personality clashes came to the forefront. We soon found out that our leading actor needed their ego massaging daily. There were also a couple of people injecting a steady stream of gossip which created a toxic environment. We then discovered one of them, a girl, was self-harming, but before we could arrange help for her, she jumped on a train and never returned. For weeks, we battled to keep the team on track but somehow the bad in the company corrupted the good. Of course, we tried our best as leaders, but eventually we had to admit the situation was irretrievable and the battle unwinnable, so time was called on that team.

I remember when we said goodbye to the remnants of the team, how disappointed I felt. They had started so well, but the team self-destructed.

It taught me a lot as a leader. I realised it is easy to see the talent of an individual, but it's about the character of the person who has got the talent that really matters. A good team must be made up of people with good characters, who are willing to serve each other and do great things together. There is simply no 'I' in team.

Question: What kind of team player are you?

Challenger

"Your father put a heavy yoke on us, but now lighten the harsh labour and the heavy yoke he put on us, and we will serve you"

(1 Kings 12:4 NIV).

(Suggested reading: the whole story: 1 Kings 1-20)

On the 27th January 1986, the NASA space shuttle *Challenger* sat on the launch pad, ready to go into space the next day. Cape Canaveral had been unusually cold that night and remained so during the morning of the blast-off. Roger Boisjoly, an engineer from the firm that built the rocket boosters, along with other engineers pleaded with NASA to delay the launch because they had serious concerns that the rubber gaskets, called O-rings, could fail at these icy temperatures. These O-rings were used as joints to seal sections of the solid rocket boosters but had never been tested at these extreme temperatures. The engineers warned of possible failure in these conditions and that the result would be catastrophic. NASA's senior managers rejected their pleas and ignored their own safety protocols.

Roger was so distressed by the decision to proceed that he chose not to watch the launch. However, millions of schoolchildren had tuned in to witness the take-off, knowing that a schoolteacher was part of the crew. Seventy-three seconds into the flight, one of the O-rings failed. Thousands of spectators and millions of children witnessed a huge explosion as the spacecraft disintegrated, killing all seven astronauts.

An investigation followed and found that NASA had developed a culture that all but ignored safety procedures in order to meet the schedules and keep politicians happy.

In today's Bible passage, we witness another explosion that changed history.

After the death of King Solomon, his son Rehoboam was to be crowned king. But before the coronation the northern tribes of Israel wanted a word with Rehoboam about some grievances. Jeroboam, an exiled former official, was the person to bring their request forward. Jeroboam presented their case to Rehoboam. He pointed out that for years the northern part of Israel had been loyal subjects to Solomon, but they had also laboured under harsh conditions.

Now they wanted to lighten their burden in exchange for their loyalty to Rehoboam.

Rehoboam consulted his father and advisors who recommend this would be a good move for the unity of the country. However, he rejected their insight and instead opted for the council of his peers, who recommended making the plight of the northern Israeli tribes even greater. It resulted in an almighty explosion and the northern tribes revolted against Rehoboam. The great kingdom disintegrated into two nations.

Like NASA, Rehoboam failed to listen and take on board wise advice.

Question: What can you, learn from these stories?

Prayer:
In the world of many sound bites, influencers and easy access for difficult issues, help me not to be tempted to listen to voices that tell me what I want to hear, but to the people who tell me what I need to hear. Surround me with good people, who give good godly advice.

Amen.

Charles Spurgeon
The Prince of Preachers
(1834 – 1892)

Born in Kelvedon, England, Charles Spurgeon spent his childhood living with his grandfather, a nonconformist minister. There a visiting itinerant evangelist prophesied over him that 'This child will one day preach the gospel to great multitudes', which was rather strange as Spurgeon had not actually made a commitment to Christ. His conversion came at the age of fifteen when he had set off to church and a terrible snowstorm descended, causing him to divert to a small Methodist chapel where a few people were worshipping. The weather also prevented the regular minister from attending. Hence, one man there, who was barely literate, delivered the sermon using the passage in Isaiah 45: 22 (KJV).

"Look unto me, and be ye saved, all the ends of the earth: for I am God, and there is none else".

This challenged Spurgeon and, for the first time, he understood that he had to look to Christ to be saved.

At seventeen, with his schooling complete, Charles moved to Cambridge but not to enter a university. A church encouraged him to preach in the surrounding countryside. He preached his first sermon to a few folks in a cottage. His gift for delivering God's word seemed mature for his years. Over the coming months, as he preached, his faith began a mini revival and his diary was filled with speaking engagements. Not long afterwards, he accepted his first pastorate at the Baptist Chapel in Waterbeach. The church quickly grew from a few to more than four hundred. Spurgeon's ability caught the attention of London's largest Baptist church. New Street Church invited him to preach a few times and within a few months, at the age of nineteen and only four years after his conversion, he was installed as the new pastor. It was at this church that Charles met his future wife. The church's glory days seemed long past, but within a short time his ability as a preacher saw the congregation outgrow the building. Construction of a new five-thousand-seater Metropolitan Tabernacle followed. While this was taking place the congregation met in Exeter Hall and the eight-thousand-seater Surrey Music Hall until the Tabernacle construction was completed in 1861.

At twenty-two, Spurgeon was already a preaching sensation. A man God used to reach out to all levels in society. Spurgeon's powerful voice, energy, and oratorical skills earned him the reputation of the 'Prince of Preachers'. He would pace the platform, acting out biblical stories, filling his sermons with sentimental tales relating to life and the Christian message. He frequently peached to audiences of ten thousand. It is estimated that ten million people heard him and he became so famous that some children believed he was the British Prime Minister. His sermons were published weekly and sold for a penny. At its peak, more than ten thousand copies of his sermons were being distributed weekly and reproduced in the London Times and New York Times.

While preaching at the Surrey Gardens Music Hall on 19th October, 1856, tragedy struck. A fire had been spotted by one of those attending and the ensuing panic and stampede left several dead. The effects of the incident left Spurgeon emotionally devastated, sending him into deep depression.

Charles was strongly opposed to slavery, seeing a slaveholder as a man stealer. This offended Southern Baptists and, as a result, sales of his sermons plummeted, and he received scores of threatening and insulting letters. Traditional Protestants labelled him a 'pulpit buffoon'. In 1864 he caused controversy with his articles about how evolutionary thinking and liberal theology threatened to downgrade the church. This protracted controversy took its toll on Spurgeon's health. He preached his final sermon to nearly three thousand six hundred at the Metropolitan Tabernacle on 7th June 1891.

After his death, his body lay in state at the Metropolitan Tabernacle and nearly sixty thousand people passed his casket to pay their respects. Some one hundred thousand lined the streets of the funeral parade. Flags flew at half-mast and shops and pubs were closed. The man known as the 'Prince of Preachers' was buried at West Norwood Cemetery London and his place of rest is regularly visited by his admirers.

Well after his passing, Charles Spurgeon's legacy continues. His involvement in the community, particularly the opening of a boys and girls' orphanage, alms houses, and the distributing of food and clothing to the poor were just one aspect of a life of dedication and service to God. One of his greatest achievements was the establishment of a bible college which opened in 1856 to train people for the ministry.

Christian Leadership – Lead by Following

"Jesus called them together and said, 'You know that those who are regarded as rulers of the Gentiles lord it over them, and their high officials exercise authority over them. Not so with you. Instead, whoever wants to become great among you must be your servant, and whoever wants to be first must be slave of all"

(Mark 10:42-44 NIV).

Christian leadership is very different from secular leadership. Jesus speaks of this 'servant-leadership'. To be a good leader means being a great follower. Unless a Christian leader is closely following Christ then how can one lead the way? The Great Commission includes the instruction 'teaching them to obey everything I have commanded you' (Matthew 28:20 NIV). So, disciple-makers must first be disciples. Leaders must first be followers.

Preachers would love to think that listeners absorb everything they say, but we say far more by the way we live. This is especially true when we are under pressure from some form of attack. The Apostle Paul said, 'Follow my example, as I follow the example of Christ'(1 Corinthians 11:1 NIV), and the same theme of being an example to be followed or a model to be imitated is repeated in Philippians 3:17 (NIV) and 4:9 (NIV); 1 Thessalonians 1:6 (NIV); 2 Thessalonians 3:7,9 (NIV). If leaders don't live what they preach, they are not Christian leaders.

Leaders follow Christ in order to lead others. The Spirit speaks to us from the Word, in our hearts, through the experiences we are going through, and through others in whom the Spirit lives. But we don't lead people by following people. Rather, we weigh up all that the Spirit says and we listen for discernment of the direction in which we should go – and hopefully people will follow us. However, sometimes they don't. How do we react then? Our responsibility is to offer a lead, but we cannot insist that people follow us. If it is our duty to offer this, when people disregard it and things go wrong – what do we do then? We pick up the pieces and continue to follow Jesus.

Peter Idris Taylor

Christian Leadership – Lead from the Front

"Follow my example, as I follow the example of Christ"
                                    (1 Corinthians 11:1 NIV).

One of the biggest problems in Christian leadership is getting people to follow you; but then, the task of Christian leadership is not getting people to follow you, but to follow Jesus. By following Jesus closely, leaders are out in front and so often are that one step ahead of those they are called to lead.

Many leaders know what it is to offer a lead and find that people just don't get it. Having once pitched an inspired idea to a leadership team only to see it was clearly going nowhere, I found, a few months later, within the same group, someone else comes up with an identical idea and everyone said, 'That's a great idea! Why hasn't anyone thought of this before?' The temptation is to point out that you gave them that idea months ago – but if we believe this is a God-inspired idea, it doesn't matter who gets the credit as long as God's will is done. (Although it would be nice for leaders if people occasionally noticed that the leader had also listened to God!). By sticking close to God and listening carefully to him leaders are often way out in front and waiting for others to catch up.

If we imagine that the vision God gives us is like Juliet on the balcony and we are a Romeo on the ground, to reach our goal we set a ladder in the right direction. Unable to take one leap from where we are to where we need to be, each rung of the ladder is a step towards our final destination. As leaders, we set a direction towards the revelation given to us. As opportunities come our way to move closer, we take those small steps. By the time the rest of the church catches up with the vision, they are already moving towards it. But sometimes being out in front is uncomfortable and can be misunderstood. The calling of God to lead is a difficult path, it has both blessings and stresses.

Paul describes the Sacrifices and Joys of leaders in Corinthians 4: 9-13 (NIV).

Peter Idris Taylor

Christian Leadership - Keep in Step

"While they were worshiping the Lord and fasting, the Holy Spirit said, 'Set apart for me Barnabas and Saul for the work to which I have called them'"

(Acts 13: 2 NIV).

Christian leaders are not just 'set apart' for God, they are often set apart from other people (Acts 13: 2 NIV; Romans 1: 1 NIV). This means that they are sometimes out of step with those they are called to lead. Moses, Elijah, and even Jesus experienced loneliness and being misunderstood in their ministry as their followers would try to bring them into line (Numbers 12: 1-2 NIV; 14: 1-4 NIV; 1 Kings 19: 9-10 NIV; Matthew 16: 23 NIV; Mark 8: 33 NIV).

Leaders have to keep in step – but not with the crowd, or those they lead, or with society as a whole. They have to 'keep in step with the Spirit' (Galatians 5: 25 NIV). Unless leaders are walking step by step with God, how can they know where they should lead others? Keeping in step means not lagging behind and not running on ahead.

Car headlights only light up the road for a short distance, yet they can lead us safely for a hundred miles. We are given enough light when we keep following in the direction that the Spirit gives us. The Spirit is never going to lead us somewhere different to that already revealed in the Word of God – the Bible, (spiritual inspiration itself). So, we keep refreshing our sensitivity to God's leadership while staying familiar with the voice of God as he speaks through his Word. All this helps us to keep in step with the Spirit even when we are out of sync with those who would try to hold us back or push us in a direction that is not of God's desire.

Peter Idris Taylor

51

Clock Hands

"Very early in the morning, while it was still dark, Jesus got up, left the house and went off to a solitary place, where he prayed"
(Mark 1:35 NIV).

A friend of mine was telling me that the large international engineering company he worked for made it compulsory that the first half an hour of the working day they were to be at their desks but do nothing other than just sit there with computers off. It was time to let the mind contemplate the challenges, dreams and creative ideas that might lie before them. I believe pen and paper was allowed, to jot down ideas. The company found that employees were more productive and creative if the mind had space rather than starting the day by firstly opening and answering lists of emails or similar mundane tasks.

Finding space and peace amongst the noise and demands of the day may seem impossible. To achieve this, you have to develop discipline, especially when it comes to creating time with God. To step out of the circle of rotating busyness takes will power that develops over time into a positive habit. This enables you to 'take five' from all the hustle and bustle and connect with God. You may say that others don't know your life, the pressures you face, the demands of family, work and church. You may feel you cannot stop, you don't have time. Actually, you are wrong; we do have the gift of time at our fingertips, but so often we will let other people, or circumstances, dictate or control the speed at which the clock hands of our life turns.

Youth with a Mission *(YWAM)* have a motto, 'To know God and to make Him known'. Even in Christian work, people can be so busy making God known, that they forget to know him. Jesus faced the demands of people following him, but he chose to find a place to stop and connect with God the Father. Being still, creating that mind space, relaxing, and topping up the spiritual, physical and emotional batteries protects us from the inevitable fatigue that can trap us in a never-ending loop steering us away from all that is good.

Jesus knew the demands of the people, yet chose to retreat, reconnect and recharge. To know God, you have to turn up and engage with him. Finding that stopping place isn't a luxury, it's a necessity. But you have to choose to make it happen.

Prayer:

In my busy world, where demands outnumber the hours, I commit myself to putting you top of my list. To commune with you before communication with others. I pray that in our time together that you will implant peace and wisdom in my soul. That I will not be a person who rushes from one thing to another in some haphazard manner but a person who brings calm and your peace into a situation. Fill me with your spirit, help me to be a beacon of hope to others in a world of cluttered diaries and frantic activity.

Amen.

Clutter

"Let us throw off everything that hinders and the sin that so easily entangles. And let us run with perseverance the race marked out for us"

(Hebrews 12:1 NIV).

Have you ever asked yourself how cluttered your life is? All that 'stuff' accumulated over time that is rarely or never used. The favourite location for these items being 'out of sight, out of mind' is the attic. This location is followed by other stashing places; cupboards, kitchens and home office areas. These are places people commonly hide items that they think may one day be of use – one day! Articles of clothing are another thing that we can become overly emotionally attached too. Garments that no longer fit are stored rather than recycled because we assure ourselves that after the next diet, they will once again be worn. Home gym equipment, for all the motivation and intent, is high on the list of dust collectors. The biggest reason people hold onto things is 'that one day I might need it'. Then there is the odd big-ticket item we store. I recently sold my beloved VW camper van because I realised despite all my plans for renovation, it was another burden on my time and another thing that would distract and hinder me from things of real value.

Emotionally, we can attach ourselves to items that are actually unhelpful from past relationships, including photos, an item of clothing, or jewellery we were given. I wonder how many marriages are cluttered and hindered by 'what if' reminders from past relationships?

Both emotional clutter and physical hoarding takes up valuable space in our life. Is it time we stopped and asked ourselves, am I holding onto things that hinder me, and that stop me creating space for the new?

Prayer:
Show me Lord the things that clutter my time and space, possessions and demands that have no real value in my life. Help me to use social media in a way that is constructive rather than a time-consuming distraction. Help me to identify the necessary from the excessive.
Amen.

Crime

"God will bring into judgment both the righteous and the wicked, for there will be a time for every activity, a time to judge every deed"
(Ecclesiastes 3:17 NIV).

Becoming a victim of crime can be a distressing experience. Even small acts of vandalism to your car may cause both inconvenience and misery, not forgetting the repair bill. Malicious scams that raid your life's savings, acts of violence, or sexual abuse can be life changing experiences for victims, leaving both physical and mental scars.

Victims of crime want the offender caught. The more serious the offence the greater the desire for retribution and justice. But what is justice? In its simplest definition, it is punishment of those found guilty of breaking the law of the land; unacceptable behaviour or wrongful action against a person(s) or a company or a nation. If something happens to us, we want the person responsible 'brought to book', to be tried and receive a punishment proportional to severity of their crime.

After the Second World War many Auschwitz guards received prison sentences for crimes against humanity, but others eluded capture. It may seem unfair that perpetrators of serious crimes can go free. A victim may feel a huge sense of injustice and that the system has let them down. How do we cope with injustice when we have been wronged: stolen from, assaulted, defrauded, suffered racism, abused, or our property/home violated? How do we stop carrying the burden of pain related to being a victim?

There is no magic answer that will bring instant pain relief or settle scores. But there is a challenge for us, to let go of what happened and start to look forward. A choice that says, I am not going to let the past wreck my future. I give the pain and the injustice up to you God, knowing you will make the final judgement on someone's life. It is you God who one day will judge my thoughts, words, and deeds.

Prayer:
Sometimes, Lord, the world seems a cruel and callous place, unforgiving and greedy, driven by want and power. I pray for those who have been unlawful in their actions towards me. I pray that you will enable me to forgive them.
Amen.

Comparison Culture

"I praise you because I am fearfully and wonderfully made; your works are wonderful, I know that full well"

(Psalm 139:14 NIV).

For three years, I studied musical theatre in an environment that was very competitive where I was also being bred into what I like to call 'Comparison Culture'. This became the catalyst to a decline in my self-esteem. Being the only Christian in college was a very lonely experience because I had no one else who understood my way of thinking or to whom I could relate.

A combination of needing to be weighed every week, using social media, being in a toxic relationship, and falling away from my faith in God, led me to having a very low opinion of myself. This affected my view of the way I looked more than anything else, but also created in me a lot of self-doubt about my capabilities in all aspects of life.

However, I was drawn to the Bible verse of the day quoted here, in particular because I felt it perfectly depicts God's love for all of us. It helps to remind us that God carefully created each one of us with a lot of thought, making no mistake with how we were formed. If we can appreciate nature in all its beauty, which is also God's creation, then why can't we appreciate ourselves?

It is time to take look at ourselves in the mirror through God eyes?

Prayer and Praise:
Thank you for making me the way I am, created in the image of God. Help me to be secure in who I am and recognise my unique attributes and strengths.

Amen.

Stephanie Wolfe

Consider it Joy

"Consider it pure joy, my brothers and sisters, whenever you face trials of many kinds, because you know that the testing of your faith produces perseverance"

(James 1:2-3 NIV).

Consider it joy...... when you're lost in the storm, struggling with life, because nothing's the norm.

Consider it joy....... when you're feeling the stress, when everything's wrong or things are a mess.

Consider it joy...... because then I'm at work, bringing good out of bad, finding gold in the dirt.

Consider it joy,....... a real chance to shine, for people around you to see that you're mine.

I'll bring light into darkness and joy into pain, you know I can do this again and again.

As you give me your tears, I'll go to great lengths, to show you for real that my joy is your strength.

Consider my joy...... receive it from me, then you'll discover how good life can be.

Marion Boyton

Cricket

How would you explain a living faith to someone with little understanding of the Christian message? Maybe it would be like explaining cricket to an American:

In cricket you have two sides,

One 'Out' in the field and the other one 'In'.

Each man in the side that's 'In' gets 'Out',

and when he's 'Out' he comes' In'.

Then, the next man goes 'In' until he's 'Out'.

When they are all 'Out',

the side that was 'Out' comes 'In'

and the side that's been 'In' goes 'Out'

and tries to get those coming 'In' 'Out'.

When both sides have been 'In'

and all the men have been 'Out'

and both sides have been 'In' and 'Out' twice

and after all the men have been 'In', including those not 'Out',

that's the end of the game - That's Cricket explained in a nutshell in plain English. Ha!

To those who have found and experienced a living faith, the message of the gospel may seem simple but for others the very concepts are alien and incomprehensible. I wonder, if you were asked to explain the 'Ins and Outs' of the basics of your Christian faith would you know what to say? Would your explanation be a game changer, and would they want to be 'In' rather than 'Out'?

David and Bathsheba

"One evening David got up from his bed and walked around on the roof of the palace. From the roof he saw a woman bathing. The woman was very beautiful, and David sent someone to find out about her. The man said, 'She is Bathsheba, the daughter of Eliam and the wife of Uriah the Hittite"

(2 Samuel 11:2-3 NIV).

I wondered what David thought when he saw Bathsheba taking a bath. Presumably he watched her for a while, admiring her womanly shape from the vantage point of his rooftop terrace; attraction becoming desire in his mind. Was Bathsheba aware of his observation? Perhaps ... perhaps not. We might wonder why she was bathing in plain sight and whether that was just the culture of the time or something more.

And when David's heart and mind turned desire into brutal lust and then into action, boy, what action it was! He wanted Bathsheba. His desire to have her had no barriers and his position as king gave him the power to manipulate the situation to fulfil his lust. Having found out more about her, she was summoned. She went. They had an illicit, one-off sexual encounter that led to a pregnancy – and a string of attempted cover-ups of the wrong-doing.

David ordered Uriah, her husband, back from the war so that he would sleep with his wife, Bathsheba. But, due to laudable loyalty to his fellow troops, Uriah wouldn't take an opportunity that could result in making it look as though he had impregnated Bathsheba. Moving forward in the story a few verses; Uriah ended up back on the front line in a premeditated fashion, and in an unsurvivable situation.

Bathsheba mourned her husband's death and was later brought to King David to be his wife. In 2 Samuel: 12 (NIV), Nathan the prophet visited David and told him of the Lord's disapproval and displeasure with David's contempt for the many blessings that David had already received from God. Even though David repented of his sin, Nathan told David that the son that Bathsheba was expecting would die. It seemed the consequences of his actions were even impacting on a young innocent individual with whom he was involved.

It is a sobering thought, how one wrongful action can have such long-term impact.

Did I Miss Anything ?

"Children are a heritage from the Lord, offspring a reward from him. Like arrows in the hands of a warrior are children born in one's youth. Blessed is the man whose quiver is full of them. They will not be put to shame when they contend with their opponents in court"

(Psalm 127: 3-5 NIV).

Spouse one:	*(Early morning)* Leaves for work early, there are reports to write, people to manage and a backlog of demanding emails to clear.
Spouse two :	*(Afternoon)* Collects child from primary school, then the evening supper to prepare.
The meal:	*(5.30pm)* Dining table set, Supper served, seats filled but one. Everyone aware of the empty place, – vacant so regularly, that it is just taken as fact, but still the questions come.
The children:	They are asking when will their father be coming home?
Soon:	You have no other reply, but you have said 'soon', too often to be believed.
Resentment:	You share your children's disappointment. You feel resentment of towards your partner, and his job that demands so much of him that he has little time for loved ones.
Bedtime:	Children's bedtime routine: clean teeth, bedtime stories. You just hope that the other half will make a cameo appearance before children enter their world of dreams
Darkness	Day fades to night. You wait alone. Still no show. They must have had another demanding day with loose ends to tie up. Once again, you feel like a lone parent.

Headlights:	Car lights illuminate the drive. You witness a tired, slightly grumpy partner arrive. The routine: just feed them, leave them for an hour in front of the television or reading social media posts.
Never forget:	The golden rule – make sure you only enter into fleeting conversation, little detail, nothing to deep, and don't ever talk about planning family life.
Work world:	Partner feels quite content in their all-consuming world of work, exhausted at times but generally fulfilled.
Isolated	You feel lonely. Married in name but isolated in reality.
Empty nest:	*(Fifteen year later)* No dependants now. Flown the nest.
Spouse one:	Career moved sideways, surpassed by a younger generation. Brave new world, hard to stay in the race.
Spouse two:	Partner home at 5.30. Meal on table. Just the two of us
Dinning table	Four chairs, Two empty.
Spouse one	For a fleeting moment, I wondered... 'Did I miss anything?'

Dilemma

"The Lord detests dishonest scales,
but accurate weights find favour with him"

(Proverbs 11:1 NIV).

A friend of mine has a dilemma about doing 'what is right' or 'saving money'. This is the situation: They have two houses; one is rented and in good condition, the other house is their home and is an ongoing renovation project. They have little spare money but a big dream for their own home.

Their dilemma; they could make some much-needed savings if they used receipts from their home restoration and 'offset' them against the costs incurred for the rented property. Basically, they would be claiming that the building materials used for their renovation were used to improve the rented property, which, obviously wouldn't be the truth. Hence, by manipulating the truth they would benefit by paying less tax.

If you found yourself in this dilemma, What would you have done?

Recently I discovered one of our voluntary team members was receiving universal credit (Government support) during her gap year with us. The principle was, team members should raise their own support and trust God to provide. The person chose not to inform the benefits office that she was now not seeking employment and was undertaking a voluntary gap year, as this would have meant her payments stopped. Ironically, the government department failed to review her case. The additional few thousand gave her a financially comfortable mission gap year compared to other team members.

Would you have contacted the benefits office, or taken the money?

The effect on our wallet challenges our integrity.

Disappointment

"Those who hope in me will not be disappointed"

(Isaiah 49: 23 NIV).

There is a 'pain gap' between our expectations and reality, its called disappointment, within that space lingers the feeling of loss and sadness. Maybe it's a relationship that has failed, a job that didn't work out, years of trying to conceive and each month the pregnancy test is negative, or an unanswered prayer for a healing. At times you may even feel God has let you down. Hopes are dashed, expectations crushed. Faith is suppressed and disappointment reinforced. Let's be real, you cannot escape disappointment in this broken world, but where can we find help in moments of discomfort and dismay?

Firstly, we must acknowledge our pain, our frustrations, the blow of disappointment. Crying to cope with despondency, sharing with others, receiving prayer and taking time to lament about the situation are all paths to healing.

Some of the Psalms are God's therapy. Maybe using some of the words from Psalm 44, Psalm 60 and Psalm 77 (NIV) can help you put your emotions into words. Denying disappointment never leads to healing.

Being let down, and finding dreams are shattered sows seeds of disillusionment. Don't let them take root in your life because they could become weeds of bitterness that will entangle you and stop you moving forward.

One of Gods promises to us is:

"Those who have hope in me will not be disappointed."

Discrimination

"My friends, as believers in our Lord Jesus Christ, the Lord of Glory, you must never treat people in different ways according to their outward appearance"

(James 2:1 GNT).

Before you read the following story I would encourage you to read the entire passage James 2.1-10 GNT for a greater overview.

In 1947, when law students Seretse Khama and Ruth Williams met at an event organised by the London Missionary Society, it was love at first sight. Initially unknown to her, he was the heir to the King of the Bangwato people, who lived in the British protectorate area of Bechuanaland (now Botswana). From the start of their relationship, they were met with hostility because he was black and she was white. Family, tribal elders, even people in the street disapproved, but more substantially, because of Seretse's future position, they faced political pressure from the British and South African governments who opposed their intended marriage. This was because it was against the newly established system of apartheid in neighbouring South Africa. Sadly, even the London Missionary Society and the Church of England helped block their church wedding, but despite this, they married at a registry office in 1948. Together, as husband and wife, they crossed the threshold but now would face a campaign to nullify and destroy their marriage. They endured years of discrimination, battling against the establishment for equality and against racial segregation.

In the Bible reading, James, a Jew, shows us that discrimination and inequality were prevalent in biblical times too: Jews and Gentiles, slaves and free citizens, male and female (Galatians 3:28 NIV); Roman citizens and non-Roman citizens, Greek speakers and non-Greek speakers, the rich and the poor etc. Interestingly, at this time there was no discrimination based on the colour of people's skin, however, history tells us that the discrimination against the poor has been in every society and age! It has always been the rich against the poor, it has never been the other way around.

The early believers lived out the unity and openness in their communities and the effect was shocking to the Roman world. People took note. James wrote to encourage them to continue living a life of impartiality because this doesn't come naturally.

In post-war Britain, the colonialist mentality and the church's backslapping supported the implementation of apartheid. I'm pleased to say that, in my lifetime, the church has changed its position and church leaders have spoken up for the abolishment of discrimination. Seretse Khama and Ruth Williams fought a battle for a better world where we have equality which isn't determined by the colour of our skin.

I wonder ... in our hearts, do we discriminate?

Do we favour the rich over the poor?

Do we favour the outward appearance over a person's heart?

Do we discriminate because of race, colour of skin or sexual bias?

This passage challenges us to choose relationship over discrimination, fellowship over lordship.

Now, ask yourself; in your life, in what areas do you discriminate?

Doing The Devil's Work

"Our struggle is not against flesh and blood, but against the ruler, against the authorities, against the power of this dark world and against the spiritual forces of the evil in the heavenly realms"

(Ephesians 6:12 NIV).

Once in our organisation there was an awful bust up over the deliverance of a staff appraisal which left an employee distraught. The appraisal, instead of empowering a good person, unfairly criticised them when the measurable evidence indicated a good employee bringing success to the charity.

The staff member submitted a complaint, raising serious concerns about the conduct of the person giving the appraisal and disputing the facts. Sadly, rather than taking the complaint seriously and self-examining their actions, the assessor simply went into self-denial mode. To give their appraisal review spiritual justification, they claimed it was soaked in prayer – so they must be right!

A situation that could have been nipped in the bud progressed to a level which was starting to damage the entire organisation. The lack of good listening skills and an honest evaluation turned into a two-year internal battle. Board members resigned from their posts, the employee became unwell and was off work for months, the charity revenue started to collapse, company moral was low and recruitment was suffering.

The situation was only resolved when the employee hired a solicitor, who,armed with ammunition of employment law and the possibility of a tribunal, finally got the management to concede and admit their failings. The employee won his fight and an out of court settlement was made. However, serious damage was done to the people involved and the charity itself.

Sadly, the real winner was the 'Devil,' who watched gleefully as in-house fighting paralysed the organisation and caused unnecessary pain and suffering which could have so easily been resolved.

Let us not do the devil's work, let us walk with humility and grace.

Prayer:

Lord Jesus, help me in my actions to be fair, just and righteous.

Help me be a person who is humble, able to review my actions when challenged, and correct them if I am wrong.

Help me not to be filled with pride, but be one who walks in your humility and grace.

Lord, help me to say the right things at the right time, to build up and empower those around me. Help me to be in tune with your Spirit, who doesn't harbour bias or prejudice.

Let me be a person of encouraging words. Help me be a person who brings peace, rather than distress. Teach me when it is right to be firm, but never bully. Help me carry words, actions and position well. Help me to never be a person who does the Devil's work or abuses a position of power.

Help me to be more like you, humble, and always in tune with your Spirit.

Amen.

Don't Let The Good Things Die

"An unmarried man concerns himself with the Lord's work, because he is trying to please the Lord. But a married man concerns himself with worldly matters, because he wants to please his wife; and so he is pulled in two directions"

(1 Corinthians 7:32-34 GNT).

Some years ago while on a two week church mission, I stayed with a young family in Dundee. They seemed like a happy couple on the surface, but after a few days of living with them, my initial impression of their perfect marriage began to fade. My first indication that all was not rosy was when I overheard the wife on the 'dog and bone' to a friend. She was bitterly complaining that her husband spent more time out at church activities than he did at home. A week later, I walked into the kitchen and found her quietly weeping at the kitchen table. It transpired that she had become lonely and felt that she had become a low priority on her husband's list of commitments. Church leadership responsibilities seemed to be top of his agenda. He would often return from work, have a meal, and rush off to some church event. His excuse for his business was that God had to be number one in his life. She found this hard to challenge – when all he was doing was for God!

While it may seem right to a person to devote a large amount of their time and energy to God. Paul makes it clear in his letter to the Corinthians that married Christians have different commitments to single Christians. Single believers are able to give their undivided attention to God's work. Married people, however, are no longer able to do this. Their interests are divided because they also have a responsibility towards their family: Whether we are married or single, we are expected to be wise stewards of our time and energy. Giving time and attention to our spouse, children, loved ones and friends is actually one way that we can please God.

Prayer:
Help me to be a wise steward of my time, loving you and those who are closest to me. Help me be a conduit of your love to those I care about. May my love for you be reflected in my love for others.

Amen.

Driven Rat

"This day I call the heavens and the earth as witnesses against you that I have set before you life and death, blessings and curses. Now choose life, so that you and your children may live and that you may love the Lord your God, listen to his voice, and hold fast to him"

(Deuteronomy 30:19-20 NIV).

There are about 2.2 rats for every person in London. That's a lot of rats running around the streets of the capital, scavenging for food and swimming in the city sewers. They say that in London, you are never more than six-foot from a rat' They've been bedding down near us in unoccupied buildings, hiding in cars, attics, under floorboards, and in cavity walls for years. Some have even made an abode under Jacuzzis. Rats are driven by three things: a supply of food, water and a place to breed. If the supply of food runs extremely low, they are so driven by their basic need that they can turn on each other in acts of cannibalism.

Mankind has similar basic needs of food, water and physical connection. Our needs are more complicated than the rats, as we have not only a physical body, but also a soul and spirit. A few years ago, Richard Foster wrote a book called *Money, Sex and Power*. He identified these three keys 'drives' that have the power to curse or to bless others.

The problem with our internal motivators is they can distort and corrupt the way we live out our lives. Money, sex and power blur the lines of righteousness and holiness. Income and profit can become more important than relationships. Power and domination can lead to unrighteous ownership and crushing of God's direction. Lust can lead to depersonalization, devouring rather than nourishing.

We may not live our lives driven by all consuming extremes of influence of money, sex and power, but we occasionally all need to stop, look in the mirror and ask, 'What drives me? What motivates my actions? How are they affecting my decision-making process? Are my actions in thought and deed self-centred and self-gratifying, rather than God-centred and servant-hearted?'

Duvet Days

"By the seventh day God had finished the work he had been doing; so on the seventh day he rested for all his work"

(Genesis 2:2 NIV).

A few years ago, I had a job as a door-to-door salesperson, which for the most part was surprisingly enjoyable and more than paid the bills. I kept a daily record of my successful sales and I noticed that they would vary from one day to another. I soon realised that if I had a spring in my step and naturally smiled, people were more ready to listen. The sign ups came at a steady pace. Contrastingly, if I was lethargic, had lost my spark, then cold calling at the door was a hard knock with little reward. The reason for this was that people buy into the sales persona more than the product.

To get to my sales pitch I had to drive half an hour which was a rather pleasant journey from Yeovil to Dorchester across the hills of Dorset. On one particular morning, I was feeling a little weary but as I did not want to let the side down, I was determined to do my bit for the area sales monthly target. On my journeys I would often listen to Radio Four and on that particular day, they were discussing 'Duvet Days'.

The core concept of 'Duvet Days' was a clause to be built into person's employment contract that allowed them some random days off to gain a little more shut eye. So, if you were over-tired and felt a few hours of snoozing under the duvet would be of benefit you were allowed to just text your manager saying, 'I am taking one of my 'Duvet Days'. Once you had done this, you could return to bed, turn off the alarm clock, and enjoy a few hours of relaxing sleep. The argument for this idea was, if people were well rested, they were more likely to be productive in the long-term. Of course, all this was backed up by various academic studies which supported the argument. As I continued to drive and listen to the rather inspiring article, I was becoming convinced this was a good idea. In fact, so much so, that I pulled the car over, turned it around and headed home for a bit more shut eye. A day of work was lost but a few more dreams gained. The rest day did me good.

I heard a minister speaking a few weeks ago during a sermon saying he hadn't had day off for four weeks. My immediate reaction was 'what an idiot!'. Working flat out all the time is no good for your physical or mental health. God never meant us to be a production line of activity. He designed us to stop, relax, reflect, rest and recover. Jesus took time away from the crowds to recover and to spend time with Father God (Luke 6:12 NIV). It is good to rest, to look back and reflect on what has been achieved and to review your work. God took time to stop and review his creation and saw that it was good, (Genesis 2:3 NIV). Rest and reflection is time for recovery.

Is it time you stopped and had a 'Duvet Day' or two, to rest, reflect and pray?

Earthquake

"For whatever is hidden is meant to be disclosed, and whatever is concealed is meant to be brought out into the open"

(Mark 4:22 NIV).

Can you imagine being the head of an organisation and receiving a confusing letter from an employee telling you their actions had secretly lost the company a substantial amount of money. In this case, it was a jaw-dropping eight hundred million or more! The confessor was Nick Leeson, a Barings Bank derivatives trader, based in Singapore. Over a period of time, he had been acting as an rogue trader, not following the company's processes and was left unsupervised by the head office in London. His fraudulent trading losses escalated. The more Mr Leeson tried to correct his failing and hide his wrong-doing, the more the situation deteriorated. Even when colleagues raised concerns, they were ignored because he was falsifying the documentation, so all looked good on paper. He still hoped to recover his losses and continued recklessly trading in a gamble to strike a lucky run and recover his position. When the Kobe Earthquake struck Japan in 1995 killing more than 6,000 people, Leeson made a last-ditch attempt to turn his losses into a profit. He bet on a rapid recovery of the Nikkei stock market, which suffered a share price collapse at the time of the earthquake. But, rather than proving itself to be a winning strategy his aggressive trading went into a tail spin of crashing losses which could no longer be hidden. These losses were now revealed in the confession letter the chairman was reading. The letter revealed a scale of damage to the bank that must have been hard to comprehend. Ultimately, the financial losses were so extensive that it led to the collapse of one of Britain's oldest banks. One man took down an institution.

The Christian church is not immune from cover-ups. From 1990 into the twenty-first century the Catholic church started to attract worldwide media attention regarding priests and ordained staff. Investigations eventually found that several cases of child abuse were either covered up or not investigated. Eventually thousands of cases of abuse spanning fifty years were uncovered. Many perpetrators were brought to justice.

At the centre of both these international stories were individuals or small groups concealing their wrong actions. I hope you are not the next Nick Leeson, or a corrupt clergyman. All of us are accountable for our actions. Cover-ups start with an individual which can then involve others.

Our actions may not create an earthquake but may produce a tremor of pain. As followers of Jesus, we are called to be a light in the darkness, a beacon in a corrupt world.

Prayer:
Lord, I pray that I will live my life worthy of your name, that my actions in word and deed will be righteous, whether dealing with people or organisations. I pray for the people who suffered sexual abuse by people that they should have been able to trust for inner healing. I pray that you will expose wrongdoing in this area and bring to justice the people who abuse their position.

Amen.

Entitlement

"Jesus said to his disciples, "If any of you want to come with me, you
must forget yourself, carry your cross, and follow me"

(Matthew 16:24 NIV).

A few years ago, I asked a friend what they needed to meet their financial
needs. What I got back was not a list of their basic requirements but a
comprehensives inventory of their 'wants.' But more alarming to me was their
ingrained sense of entitlement that their wants should be met. An expectation
of demand: 'I am entitled too'.

Entitlement is an assumption that we deserve certain paybacks, rights,
recognition, privileges, positions of reward. It is a trait that is often learnt in
childhood and becomes embedded within us. It manifests itself and blinds us to
the fact there is a chasm between 'wants' and 'needs'. This doesn't mean that a
person lives in total self-absorption, but it does mean that perhaps given the
opportunity, their personal agenda of entitlement will surface. The belief that
one is 'inherently deserving' cannot stay suppressed forever. Eventually, the
'ME,ME' rights of entitlement emerge for all to see.

Christ challenges our view of ourselves. What are we living for? How will we
live our lives? God's word challenges our perceived rights to have more than
we need. He confronts those embedded traits of the privileged and perceived
self-importance. He promises to meet our needs but may ask us to put aside
those unnecessary things that we hanker for. Christ invites us to join him on
the road of self-denial and sacrifice; an adventure discovering life, serving
others without gain and viewing life from the other side of the chasm.

Eric Liddell (1902-1945)
Part 1: The Flying Scotsman

"Those who honour me I will honour"

(1 Samuel 2:30 NIV).

Paris Olympics 1924: The starting pistol cracked, echoing around the stadium as Eric Liddell pounded the track with his slightly ungainly manner in the 400-metre final. To the astonishment of the crowd, he flashed past the two hundred metre mark at 22.2 seconds, three metres clear of his nearest rival. Those watching must have thought that no one could run four hundred metres flat out and not fade in the home straight. On the final corner, another runner began to make ground on him, and then incredibly from somewhere Liddell summoned up hidden reserves of stamina. He flung his head back and put on a spurt. The crowd were on their feet cheering madly as he ripped through the tape claiming the Olympic title in a record time of 47.6 seconds, five metres clear of any rival.

The win was a remarkable achievement because he had switched events to run the four hundred metres rather than run in his favoured one hundred metres because the race fell on a Sunday. He was a staunch believer in the Sabbath, and he would not sacrifice his principles for the sake of a gold medal, so he refused to participate in the one hundred metre heats. He believed 'Those who honour God will be honoured', and his way of honouring God was to Keep the Sabbath as his 'God' day.

Eric gives us an example of someone sold out for Christ, a person willing to stand up for Godly principles. Following Christ could have cost him the chance to compete in the Olympic games when he refused to run on a Sunday. Sunday was time for God. A time for rest and recovery. 1.

Nearly a century later society has changed. Working patterns are more flexible, shopping more accessible. We have a long list of options to pick from when it comes to what we do with our time ... what we watch and when we watch it ... where and when we might decide to go somewhere. But in all our choices have we included the Sabbath? Or to us is that now just another day? Have we allowed there to be a gradual erosion of our 'God' day so that it has just become like any other day of the week.

What does the Sabbath mean to us? Does it change the way we live our life?

1. Ref: Magnusson, Sally, 1981, *The Flying Scotsman.*

Eric Liddell
Part 2: To China

"Forgetting what is behind and straining toward what is ahead, I press on toward the goal to win the prize for which God has called me heavenward in Christ Jesus"
(Philippians 3:13-14 NIV).

After his Olympic triumph Liddell studied Theology in Edinburgh with the aim of returning to his place of birth, China. Liddell wanted to follow in his parent's footsteps, they had been missionaries in China. On his departure a large crowd gathered at Edinburgh's Waverley Station, cheering and singing hymns from the platform. Behind him, he left a stream of tempting job offers, including lucrative top-drawer teaching posts.

Arriving in Tianjin, China, in 1925 he stepped into a country were the National Government (Kuomintang) were battling warlords. They were soon to be in a civil war fighting the communists. It was a powder-keg explosive environment.

Liddell's first job as a missionary was as a teacher with the aim of promoting the Christian faith to students. He would spend 12 years in Tianjin, where he would preach a non-political salvation. His quiet confidence came from his self-discipline and hourly morning prayer times.

Under missionary rules no single man was allowed to court – accompany a single girl by themselves. Hence, when Eric took a liking to a young woman, called Florence Mackenzie ten years his junior, he had to invite not only her but her friends under the disguise of various social activities. When he proposed to her, she was quite stunned but accepted immediately. But it would be four years from engagement to the wedding. She returned to her native country, Canada to complete her nursing training. Eric took some furlough in Scotland, and in June 1932 was ordained. Upon reuniting in Tianjin they were married on 27th March 1934. During their time in Tianjin, they had two children. Family life was happy.

For all his success on the racetrack, Eric was not driven by fame and the opportunities it brought to him, but by a deep calling of God. A sense that God had a different purpose for his life. A change of direction in his life made the appeal of staying in England a dim prospect compared to the mission God had embedded in his spirit. Eric left for China as a single man, and on route he found love and gained a wife and created a family. Finding love was not his motivation for going, it was a blessing for following Christ. When following God's lead, we should do it with a Godly motivation to serve God that bears no sub agenda. Eric went to China for the love of God not to find a wife.

Eric Liddell
Part 3: Complete Surrender

"Therefore, I urge you, brothers and sisters, in view of God's mercy, to offer your bodies as a living sacrifice, holy and pleasing to God — this is your true and proper worship"

(Roman 12:1 NIV).

From 1931 the Civil war in China between the Communist Red army and the Chinese Nationalists had been overshadowed by the Japanese invasion of north-eastern China and the destruction of vast sways of Shanghai. Tianjin was unaffected by the battles to the north or south of it, but soon the turmoil of war would split the Liddell family up forever. In July 1937 Japan launched a full-scale invasion of China and the once-waring Chinese fractions formed an alliance to fight the Japanese. The Shadow of war affected the whole country, so the British government advised British nationals to leave. Eric felt compelled to stay but it was decided that his expectant wife and their two children would leave for Canada by ship. At the port Eric hugged his wife and children, waved them off, naïvely not realising that this was to be their final goodbye.

Without his family and the increasing control of the cities by the Japanese. Eric found himself at a loose end and dedicated himself to writing a manual for Chinese pastors. The situation took a dramatic turn when the Japanese attacked Pearl Harbour in 1941. This brought further restriction of movement on all Westerners. In 1943 he found himself with thousands of allied nationals forced onto trains which travelled for a whole day to reach Weihsien Internment Camp.

The camp's compound walls had electrified wires and guard towers. Men, women and children lived in a constant state of semi-starvation and poor sanitation. There were twenty-three toilets for eighteen hundred people and limited water supply for the open showers. As they were not classified as prisoners of war but 'Civil Internees' apart from daily 'roll calls' the inhabitants had the freedom to administer their own affairs and camp committees soon organised work duties. Tension arose between various groups; the Christians were unpopular because of their sessions of praying at night and their morning singing. While there was tension within the camp, the good news was that there was little harassment from the guards Now in his mid-forties, Eric arrived at the compound and was assigned to the school to teach Maths and Science. He also coordinated camp sports, acted as warden for two housing blocks and put in charge of Christian fellowship. However it was his acts of kindness beyond his duty, that made him stand out. He played board games with the children, helped to carry coal for the older people. His selflessness stood out as a positive Christian witness. Eighteen months of interment passed taking its toll on Eric. Constantly hungry and now unwell, the strong fit man's flame had diminished to an ember. Experiencing agonising headaches and poor movement he was unable to work. He was to be diagnosed with a brain tumour. On his last day on this earth, he seemed to discover his smile and wrote down phrases from his favourite hymn *Be still, my soul.* His last words were witnessed by a nurse, *'Complete surrender'* he said. Then he had a convulsion and slipped into a coma from which he would not recover. Eric Liddell died on 21st February 1945, five months before liberation.

Question: What does complete surrender mean to us?

Fear

"When I said 'My foot is slipping", your unfailing love, Lord, supported me. When anxiety was great within me, your consolation brought me Joy."

(Psalm 94:18-19 NIV)

Once I had snowboarding lessons and after completing a nervous two days of instruction, I could stay on the snowboard and turn in the direction I wanted to go. By the time I completed the short course, I was able to snowboard down a moderate slope successfully. The problem was my ability seemed inconsistent from one day to the next. If I started well in the morning and managed to negotiate the first piste without falling I relaxed and enjoyed the ride and all the technical things came naturally, but if I face-planted myself into the snow, my confidence ebbed away rapidly. Fear was overwhelming and the possibility of fun and success was replaced with anxiety over the possibility of injury and pain.

Fear and anxiety is a part of being human and can be the first line of defence against dangerous situations. But extreme fear can also be a crippling emotion that continues to play in the background and can become quite overwhelming. It can steal our joy of life and rob us of inner peace. The heightened awareness of perceived danger can paralyse people from interacting with the world. Some suffer from anxiety in social situations or have a need for everything to be in order, or to practice extreme cleanliness in order to be able to relax.

So how do we cope with fear and anxiety? First, I want to say, God has the answer. Secondly, I want to say the answer may not be as straightforward as the laying on of hands, prayer, or meditating over a bible verse a well-meaning friend has given you. Of course, all of these can be transforming, but for many the path to living a less anxious life is a difficult journey. It may involve prayer, medication or counselling. Any of these routes may be the means by which God uses to bring more healing and freedom.

Two things that help me are to know that God has created a natural order; the sun always rises and sets, and seasons come and go, and I rest assured in this – that I am made in his image and am valued for who I am. I don't have to pretend with God, I can relax in both the security of the daily order God has provided in the universe, and in the fact that I know I am loved.

As for snowboarding, if I can learn to go with the flow, then life is good and I am surrounded by beauty that calms the spirit.

Prayer:

(For those who suffer anxiety)

Lord, sometimes I am overwhelmed by anxiety and fear.

Help me find the right pathway to greater freedom.

Bring people into my life that empower me to live as you intended.

Help me find peace for my inner turmoil.

Thank you for making me your child

Amen.

(For those praying for others)

Lord I lift up my friend *(Name)* please bring them peace, security and the support their need to deal with fear and anxiety.

Help them to live a more stress-free life, bring calm thoughts and serenity to their being.

God fill them with your spirit, bring peace in their noise of uncertainty

Amen.

Fighting Against Injustice

"But let justice roll on like a river"

(Amos 5.24 NIV).

How do we respond to injustice? Some of us will devote immense energy defending the oppressed, fighting injustices in society, trying to make a difference to other people's lives – which some have found success in doing.

In Britain in the early twentieth century, the Suffragettes fought through protests, strikes and logical arguments, for the right for women to have the vote. In South Africa, Nelson Mandela fought for the abolition of apartheid. Organisations such as Amnesty International stand up for humanity and human rights. However, for most of us, even to consider donating this amount of energy to a cause is unrealistic. Our diaries are packed with work and family commitments. But, even in our busy lives, there are things we can do. If we have the financial means, we can donate to organisations that feed the hungry, stand up for the oppressed and lobby for righteousness. We can be a part of that change being made.

You could be that person to support a colleague in a challenging situation – someone who 'stands in the gap' when inappropriate conduct has occurred or unreasonable pressure has been put on someone by others.

Today, I challenge you: if you see something that seems like a form of injustice, don't sit on the side-line watching. Step out and be a voice. Bring righteousness into the situation. By doing something, something may be achieved. By doing nothing, nothing will be achieved.

Prayer:

Lord I pray that during this day you will give me eyes that see injustice and the wisdom to know how to respond. I pray that I will make a small difference to someone's life. Please use me Lord to be a person who does not stand on the side-lines ignoring, but engages.

Amen.

Friendship

Have you ever thought about the kaleidoscope of people you come into contact with on a weekly basis? Why you are drawn to some, respect or admire others, but distrust certain individuals? What are the characteristics of the people who bring a bit of sunshine into your life? Are they caring, do they give good advice, listen or help in the time of need? Or does simply their sense of humour jolly you along? I have a post card that I have kept for years. It says, 'Good friends are hard to find'. How true that is for many of us, we may build good relationships with colleagues, close church friendships and pals we play tennis with... but who would come round when things really go wrong – when you need someone after you've lost your job, or your marriage has fallen apart, or a family member has passed away? We can be quick to post a sympathetic comment on Facebook but to ring up, turn up, even bring a meal around, how many of us would really do that?

There are great examples of friendships in the Bible (1 Samuel 18:1-5 NIV). The friendship between David and Jonathan, and Ruth and Naomi. The men's relationship was a covenantal relationship; a deep one of brotherly love in which each, on different occasions, would stand up and serve the other (1 Samuel 19:1-7; 23:15-18 NIV). The friendship of Ruth and Naomi was also one of deep commitment; Ruth refused to leave Naomi's side, 'Where you go I will go, and where you stay I will stay. Your people will be my people and your God my God, ' (Ruth1:16 NIV).

The question is what kind of friend are you? A comment poster on Facebook; one who can stand in the gap? Or a person willing to give care, have a laugh, deliver supportive words of advice? We all need friends, but good two-way relationships are hard to find. Maybe to find a friend you have to be a friend, and at times that means walking with them and sharing their journey as they share yours.

Ruth walked that extra mile. Could you?

Prayer:
Lord, help me not to be so self-consumed by my world that I become oblivious to the need of others. Help be a vessel that reflects your love. Help me be a person who brings sunshine into the lives of others.

Amen.

(Suggested reading: Ruth 1:1-1 NIV)

Getting to the Full Stop

"Let everyone be subject to the governing authorities, for there is no authority except that which God has established. The authorities that exist have been established by God"

(Romans 13:1 NIV).

This is the scenario: There is an almighty bust up between some believers, which, if left unresolved, could have both financial and practical consequences. Both parties believe they are right and antagonism has now broken out. The situation is a deadlock. No one is listening or willing to compromise. How do we find a way forward?

Ideally, following God's 'road map of conflict resolution' in Matthew 18.15-19 (NIV), would bring closure. But what happens if a conflict persists and the church does not have either the expertise, the capacity or determination to resolve the dispute?

I am sad to say, an option could be to employ a solicitor. This doesn't mean you will end up in court or at a tribunal. Solicitors will evaluate the case against the backdrop of the law of the land. Their council may suggest a compromise or a settlement agreement or even advise you to drop the case. If no resolution is found it could lead to a court case, and the court verdict brings closure.

Should Christians use the legal system? The Bible does not say Christians should never go to court. In today's passage we read that God has established legal authorities to bring judgement. The apostle Paul used the legal system as a vehicle for gaining his freedom. In fact, have you ever considered the amount of times Paul found himself in court? God has ordained governments with the right to establish a legal framework, bring justice to protect the innocent, and resolve disputes.

As Christians we must do everything in our power to live in peace with each other. Demonstrate humility and forgiveness, be willing to compromise and pray blessings on our foe. Sometimes, when all else fails legal action may be our only route to closure and justice. However, we need to remember the longer we remain head-to-head with one another, the more we have become distracted from the battle of advancing the Kingdom of God.

Prayer:

Lord, in my dealings, help me to be fair, just, and righteous. Help my relationship to always be open, friendly and honest. Let me not become stubborn, obstinate, or revengeful. Help me address problems early and solve them well for your glory.

Amen.

George Müller
(1805 -1898)

George Müller was a Christian preacher from Germany and founder of several Bristol Orphanages. He also established 117 schools and offered Christian education to more than 120,000 children. He was a founding member of the Plymouth Brethren Movement.

This is the inspirational story of a young man who was transformed from leading a life of wild living to man of God.

At the age of ten, George had developed the habit of stealing. Four years later his life was turned upside down when his mother died. As he grew into a young man, his behaviour became more reckless. On one sinful pleasure trip he stayed at several hotels without paying the bills, this led to him being arrested and spending ten days in prison. On another occasion, George arranged a trip to Switzerland with his friends. They obtained their passports using forged letters from parents ... which George wrote! He also manipulated the trip finances, charging his friends more so he didn't have to pay as much.

Ironically, his father urged him to attend university and become a clergyman. He did this, not for the reason of serving God, but to secure a career and a comfortable lifestyle. Whilst studying at university, during the semester break he continued his wayward activities which knew few moral boundaries. By the age of twenty his wild living gave him little satisfaction and he realised that unless he reformed his behaviour, no parish would ever employ him as a priest.

A Christian friend invited him to a gathering of believers where they sang hymns, prayed, and studied the Bible. Their Christian joy, their obvious love for others and their faith made a deep impression on him. Unbeknown to himself, the Holy spirit had started to work in his life, and he felt an inward happiness after attending the meeting. Suddenly, the word 'God' became interesting to him. However, he kept company with his drinking pals and his behaviour trait of lying continued. After some months of reading the word of God, and with the support from fellow brethren, he reached a place where he could fully give himself to the Lord. George recounts, that the peace of God which passes all understanding filled his life in a moment of full surrender to Christ.

Müller desired to serve as a missionary and an opportunity in England came up where he laboured among the Jews in London. From there he moved to

Devon and became the minister at Shaldon Chapel. He married Mary Groves and together they took the bold step of receiving no salary and living by faith. It was a time when God blessed them abundantly and taught them to trust Him for daily provision.

From Devon they moved to Bristol on 25th May 1832 where George began working at the Bethesda Chapel. There he set up schools for boys and girls, giving them a spiritual foundation for life. The Lord impressed on him plans to establish an Orphan house. Unbeknown to him this would be a journey of prayer, continuous trials, faith, and God provision. In 1836 the Müller's own house became an orphanage for thirty girls. This ministry was to expand considerably over the years to five houses with a capacity for two thousand children. Young people left the orphanages with an education, two changes of clothing and a Bible. Müller never sought donations but relied on God's provision for the needs of all the institutions. Often timely unsolicited donations for food would arrive only hours before they were desperately needed to feed the children before supplies ran out. Once the milk cart broke down in front of the orphanage, thus giving them fresh milk. Another time, a baker knocked on the door with fresh bread just in time for breakfast.

After the death of his first wife in 1870. He married again just a year later to Susannah Sanger. Together, in 1875, at the age of seventy-one he embarked upon seventeen years of preaching tours. This took him to forty-two countries, speaking to over three million people, and travelling over two hundred thousand miles, which was some achievement in those pre-aviation days.

The wild boy and petty thief who's life was turned around by the saving power of God changed thousands of lives. For all his achievements, it was hours of prayer behind closed doors that was the hallmark of his life – the boiler room that fuelled his mission.

George Müller died on the 18th of March 1898, aged 92.

Glass Bridge

"And without faith it is impossible to please God, because anyone who comes to him must believe that he exists and that he rewards those who earnestly seek him"

(Hebrews 11:6 NIV).

In the Piyan mountains, near Longjing, China, there is a suspension footbridge bridge that spans 430 metres across a canyon. A walkway spanning a ravine isn't particularly unusual, but the Longjing bridge poses a unusual challenge for those crossing it. Its construction is irregular; instead of having a solid floor that blocks the view below, the floor pane is constructed from interlinked glass panels. This means you can gain an amazing view of the rocky gorge 100 metres below. The challenge for those attempting to walk across is that the transparency of the concave section confuses the senses and what our brains perceive as safe. We have become accustomed to solid walkways that obscure danger and we have learnt to trust the engineering. But seeing the danger below means stepping out in faith, trusting that the designers have got their calculations right.

On our Christian walk, faith is a key element. One of the first steps believers take is accepting Jesus Christ as God's son. Another is to have faith and trust in the Bible and its core message of salvation.

Christian faith is an action taken in response to God's view on a matter. Like the glass bridge, you have to have faith in the creator to cross from one side to the other. To develop as a believer, you have to step out of your comfort zone. The challenge is putting one foot in front of the other when it is easier to stay on ground you know. Stepping out in faith into the unknown may seem uncomfortable and even terrifying, but as you walk in faith you will come to enjoy aspects of the view along the way.

Without faith it is impossible to please God.

God-centred Worship

"Therefore, I urge you, brothers, and sisters, in view of God's mercy, to offer your bodies as a living sacrifice, holy and pleasing to God—this is your true and proper worship. Do not conform to the pattern of this world but be transformed by the renewing of your mind. Then you will be able to test and approve what God's will is – his good, pleasing, and perfect will"

(Romans 12:1- 2 NIV).

I love this verse and it has been significant for me in my journey of getting closer to God. I am passionate about worship – particularly sung worship as that is how I spend much of my time around church. There are times when I have fallen into the trap of thinking that singing together is the complete extent of what worship means which has sometimes led to my feelings of 'whether worship was good or not'. Do people respond well to the singing ...?

These pitfalls lead to only one thing – making the main thing *not* the main thing. It puts me at the centre instead of putting God at the centre.

What I love about this passage and the cry from Paul is he is saying, offer your bodies as a living sacrifice – this is your true and proper worship. In Greek the word for worship used here is 'latreian' which is translated as service. For Paul, worship is not about a moment of singing on a Sunday morning in a room together with others, it is a lifestyle of service and sacrifice to God. He goes on to say 'do conform to the pattern of this world but be transformed by the renewing of your mind'. I wonder how much the pattern of the world becomes about putting me at the centre, allowing everything to revolve around my choices, my decisions, my preferences, and my feelings.

I love sung worship and believe it is one of the most grounding moments in my life where I stop and say 'Jesus this time is yours, here I am.' I want to be someone who lives a life of service every day where everything I do reflects that same attitude.

What does it look like for you today to offer your body as a living sacrifice in everything you do? What do you need to do today to make sure you don't become the centre of your world and God stays the main thing?

Joe Hardy

Grab The Turkey

'Life does not consist in an abundance of possessions'

(Luke 12:15 NIV).

I once was listening to a radio programme about house fires; what you should do and what people actually did. The official fire brigade advice includes: Try not to panic! *(My house is on fire, but I am not panicking ... really!)*

- Tell everyone in the household to use the pre-planned escape route to get out the building as quickly as possible.

- Stay low, or crawl on the floor if the area is full of smoke as the air is clearer and more breathable lower down.

- Don't stop to collect any valuables or possessions.

- Don't stop to look for pets. *(Bye hamster, nice knowing you).*

The programme then went on to explore what people actually did. The good news is that most people did successfully evacuate the building. However, there was a strong tendency to ignore the warning of collecting possessions or looking for pets. In most cases people evacuating a house filling with smoke had to grab something as a last desperate defiant act before everything was lost. A lot of people saved wedding albums or family photos or a favourite book. Items that people had their closest association with were snatched on exit.

But, when people go into panic mode, they can act irrationally. The programme told a story of a lady who, out of desperation to save something, grabbed the turkey out of the oven before exiting the building.

In an age where we can define ourselves by possessions, it's worth pausing and asking oneself, if it all went up in smoke, what would you save, and why?

Grace, Glorious Grace

"For sin shall no longer be your master, because you are not under the law, but under grace"

(Romans 6:14 NIV).

The impact of discovering God's grace and the outworking of it can be totally life changing. A few years ago, I met a lady called Grace, whose story was complicated. As a young woman in her twenties, she became a prostitute working at the high-end of the market, escorting wealthy men and staying in top London hotels. However, there was something missing; she had an emptiness inside which was mostly suppressed by her lavish lifestyle and the use of drugs. Her dependence on drugs meant she was spending everything she earned. Eventually, her lifestyle started spiralling out of control. The years of selling herself and her drug dependence started to catch up and the deep -buried inner emptiness slowly crept to the surface. She was starting to free-fall into her pit of self-destruction. Her parachute strings of dependence on men and their money were slowly being cut, one-by-one. Someone who was once wanted, was now no longer in demand. Other young attractive women were replacing her. She now realised the lie she had been living.

Her value as a person had not been measured in 'what she was', but in what she could do for men. And, as the reality of the ground came rushing towards her, she knew the crash landing was going to be painful. If she was to survive it at all she knew she had to 'Call out to God.'

The reality is that she *did* crash but something had changed. Godly people came into her life and, with unconditional love and care, she found the life-changing power of the Holy Spirit. Slowly, she came to realise that she was a valued child of God, one created in his image. Her value was not dependent on the service she could give, but on who she was as a whole person. With the power of the Holy Spirit and support, she managed to kick the drug habit.

Of course, not everything went totally smoothly. She married, but this only lasted a few years. The collapse was partly due to their physical relationship. In the failure and shame of an interesting past and a broken marriage, she found God's grace and battled valiantly against the effects the past had on her life. Today, she is a person who radiates God's love, and now, a new story is being written. Grace found 'transforming Grace'.

Hills

"For God so loved the world that he gave his one and only Son, that whoever believes in him shall not perish but have eternal life"

(John 3: 16 NIV).

When I moved to the Somerset town of Yeovil from Essex, there was something I immediately noticed as being very different from home... hills!

Walking to work, I found myself amazed at how far I could see. There were views that I'd normally only get when we went on holiday, and I marvelled at them. I took photos and praised God for how wonderful his creation was!

Over time, I got used to the hilly landscape. Seeing the fields in the distance or far-off street lights at night didn't surprise me anymore. I went back to my habit of dawdling along, staring at the ground,

But recently, with the autumn leaves falling to the ground in their spectacular display of fiery colours, I couldn't help but notice the beauty of nature, even when looking at the ground! It made me look up again and remember just how incredible God's world is.

I think a similar thing can happen with faith sometimes.

It's easy to get used to the idea that God loves us, isn't it? Some of us have been taught 'Jesus loves you' and have been reciting John 3:16 (NIV) from such a young age that we can forget what it truly means. We can get used to the beauty of God and what he has done for us, just like I got used to the beauty of nature. It's great to remind ourselves of how indescribably good God is and how much he loves us. Let's not miss out on the blessings he has for us just because we are not looking for them.

Joanna Hodgson

Hindrance

"Keep watch over yourselves and all the flock of which the Holy Spirit
has made you overseers..."

(Acts 20:28 NIV).

One of the greatest hindrances to fulfilling God's plan for your life is not
others, it is yourself, your hidden agendas and ambitions.

Being a follower of Christ means a real change in mindset; to live you have to
die to self; to lead you have to be a follower; to be first you have to be last; to
become full you need to be empty; to be strong you need to acknowledge your
weaknesses; to be brave you need to have the fear of God and to be wise you
need wisdom from many advisors.

To adopt the mantle of Christ and be a follower of Christ challenges the way
we live our life. We soon find out that within us there is a resistance of 'self'. An
obstruction called 'self-determination' and a placard that reads, 'I want to be in
control'. We will become a follower of Christ, *but* we want to rewrite some of
the terms and conditions. And if life isn't quite going as planned, it is not long
before the 'I want/I need' child within us surfaces. This is followed by the
emerging voice of blaming others and dissatisfaction with work, the church,
marriage, family relationships ... the system.

Without realising it, we become our own barrier to preventing God from
working in our lives. We become the hindrance to God's blessing on our lives
and others.

That is why this verse is so important:
'... keep watch over yourself...' (Acts 20:28 NIV).

I Am Available
(A prayer)

Use me, God.
Show me how to take who I am, who I want to be,
and what I can do.
And use it for a purpose
greater than myself.

I Am Who I Am

"Who do you say I am?"

(Mark 8:29 NIV).

Rowan Atkinson, (RA) the actor who plays Mr Bean, tells the story of being half recognised while waiting for car parts at a garage. Another customer, who is also waiting, approaches him.

Man: Excuse me, has anyone ever told you that you are the absolute spitting image of Mr Bean.

RA: Well actually, I am the actor who plays Mr Bean.

Man: (*Laughing and not believing*) I bet you wish you were.

Then a bizarre conversation erupts, where Rowan tries to convince the man that he is actually the person who plays Mr Bean. The more Rowan tries, the less the man believes him. The man keeps going on about how uncanny that he looks like Mr Bean and then suggests that Rowan take on some 'Look-alike work', saying he could make an absolute fortune by doing stag nights and hen nights as Mr Bean. The conversation continues with Rowan insisting he is the actor who plays Mr Bean but with no success. The man starts to get annoyed that this person before him has the audacity to actually claim to *be* Mr Bean when he was convinced he definitely was not.

Surprisingly, Jesus and Rowan Atkinson have something in common, neither were recognised for who they were.

When Jesus asked his disciple who the people thought he was the reply was a rather mixed bag, they told him that some said he was Elijah, others said he was one of the other prophets and others claimed he was John the Baptist. Then Jesus asked his disciples directly who they thought he was?
"You are the Messiah," they replied.

Those closest to Jesus were able to reconcile him as the Messiah, the Son of God. One of the challenges we face today is recognising Jesus in our busy lives. Hearing The Messiah's voice is knowing God's word. Dare I say it, the rounds of Christian conferences can seem more exciting than the daily devotional or personal Bible study. To identify the true voice of the Messiah communicating with us, we need to know his living word in us. It's too easy to rely on the entourage of motivational speakers and well known charismatic preachers. However, we mustn't neglect that personal connection with God so that we can truly recognise who Jesus is.

To know Jesus is to walk with him daily as the disciples did.

Prayer:
Lord give me the gift of discernment, the ability to recognise your voice in a busy world, and through the crowded arena of platform speakers.
Holy Spirit, implant in me a desire to know your word that brings the life, truth and hope in times of happiness and of struggle.
I want to see and know you Jesus.
Amen.

Martin Luther King Jr.

Iceberg – The John Harper Story
(29 May 1872 – 15 April 1912)

From an early age John Harper seemed to have a near deadly relationship with water. At the age of two and a half, he fell into a well and only survived because his mother resuscitated him. Other watery close calls experienced included surviving being swept out to sea in his thirties, and an incident on board a leaking ship in the Mediterranean that was on the point of sinking. But this was nothing compared to what he would face on a cold night in the North Atlantic Ocean.

John was brought up in a Christian family in Scotland and at fourteen made his own confession of faith. He embraced Christianity with enthusiasm, and by the age of eighteen he was preaching on the streets while supporting himself with manual jobs. His passion for the word of God and his desire to evangelise was spotted, and in 1897 he became the pastor of a little church in Glasgow. Under his influence the church attendance grew from a mere twenty-five to over five hundred over thirteen years. He also travelled throughout Britain and Ireland preaching.

During this time, he married Annie, who bore him a little daughter called Annie Jessie (Nana). Sadly, the marriage ended prematurely when Annie died in childbirth. The following year, in the autumn of 1911 he was a guest speaker at the Moody Church in Chicago. The following autumn he was invited back to minister again.

To undertake this American invitation, he bought second class tickets (£33) on the Titanic liner for himself, his daughter and his sister. The vessel's scale was truly something to marvel. One thing that did not happen on the first day of sailing was the customary lifeboat practice. What could stop a ship like this, surely it was unsinkable? Unknown to this Baptist minister, he would be sailing into history later that night.

Early that evening, John put his daughter to bed and kissed her goodnight. At 11:40pm a sudden vibration and scraping sound was heard and felt by some of the passengers. It soon became apparent that the ship had been mortally wounded in a collision with an iceberg and was sinking. Calls to vacate the cabins were given and passengers were to man the lifeboats. John awakened his beloved daughter and immediately took her to lifeboat 13. It is said he bent down to kiss his precious little girl and made sure both she and her sister were helped safely into the boat.

The last sighting of Harper was of him preaching the message of salvation to the desperate survivors as he swam about the wreckage of the sunken ship surrounded by lifeless bodies, frantically, asking survivors to accept Jesus as their savour. Harper even gave his own life jacket to a young man, who initially turned down the invitation to believe in Christ. Harper said, 'You need this more than I do', and after giving him the life jacket proceeded to swim to others to tell them about Christ. A few minutes later, Harper swam back through the dark icy waters to reach the young man and he succeeded in leading him to salvation. Exhausted in the cold water, hypothermia set in and his body succumbed to the elements and passed beneath the waves. His body was never found.

Four years later, at a survivors' meeting, a young man, who managed to stay afloat by climbing on debris from the Titanic, stood up and with tears in his eyes recounted how John Harper had led him to Christ. It was said that John's last words were:

'Believe in the Lord Jesus and you will be saved.'

(Acts 16:31 NIV)

It Is Well With My Soul
Horatio Gates Spafford (1828 – 1888)

Horatio Spafford was a successful Christian lawyer and welfare businessman in the late eighteenth century and lived in the 'Windy City' of Chicago. Although prosperous, he and his wife Anna were not immune from tragedy. In 1871, the Great Chicago Fire ripped through the wooden structure of the city destroying vast swathes of it, literally sending much of his investments up in smoke. While the impact was hard on their family, the fire had made one in three homeless in the city. For the next two years, Horatio and Anna worked amongst the refugees of Chicago. For some respite they travelled to England for a holiday and to follow the preacher D.L. Moody as he toured England. However, just before they set sail, Horatio had to stay behind and tie up some business dealings. He persuaded his wife and four daughters to take the voyage to England, promising to catch another sailing soon which would reunite them.

His wife and children boarded the single propeller steamship with sails, the *Ville Du Havre*. Tragedy again was to descend on the family when their ship was struck in the mid Atlantic Ocean by an iron clipper, the *Loch Earn*. The damage was so catastrophic that the *Ville Du Havre* started to sink. Desperately passengers struggled to move towards the lifeboats, which because they had recently been repainted were stuck fast to the deck. Suddenly, the sound of the cracking of the ship's mast was heard, shortly before it came crashing down, crushing people to death. Within minutes the ship started to break in two. Struggling in the freezing water Anna tried in desperation to cling to one of her daughters, but the turbulent waters pulled them apart. Then, for a moment, there was hope as she grabbed the edge of her daughter's nightgown, only for the waves to cruelly wrench them apart forever. The other daughters, it is understood reached a working lifeboat, only for them to lose their grip and fall into the black sea of death. Within twelve minutes SS *Ville Du Havre* had sunk with the loss of 226 souls. Of the eighty seven who survived, Anna was rescued by the crew of The *Loch Earn,* semi-conscious, floating on a piece of debris.

Reaching England, she telegrammed Horatio, informing him that all four daughters were lost. He boarded a ship from New York to England. On the way over, the captain called Horatio to the deck, and he was informed, according to captains' calculation, that this was where the *Ville du Havre* had sunk, and his daughters were lost. Horatio returned to his cabin and wrote the following hymn / song worth meditating over.

When peace, like a river, attendeth my way,
When sorrows like sea billows roll;
Whatever my lot, Thou has taught me to say,
It is well, it is well, with my soul.

It is well, with my soul,
It is well, with my soul,
It is well, it is well, with my soul.

Though Satan should buffet, though trials should come,
Let this blessed assurance control,
That Christ has regarded my helpless estate,
And hath shed His own blood for my soul.

(Refrain)

My sin, oh, the bliss of this glorious thought
My sin, not in part but the whole,
Is nailed to the cross, and I bear it no more,
Praise the Lord, praise the Lord, O my soul!

(Refrain)

And Lord, haste the day when my faith shall be sight,
The clouds be rolled back as a scroll;
The trump shall resound, and the Lord shall descend,
Even so, it is well with my soul.

It is well, with my soul,
It is well, with my soul,
It is well, it is well, with my soul.

Horatio Gates Spafford 1873

I'm Off

"We know that suffering produces perseverance; perseverance, character; and character, hope"

(Romans 5:3-4 NIV).

Have you ever known anyone who just walked out? It could be in a relationship, a job or a volunteering situation? It could be after an argument or a dispute over money – the employee who finds a better position, or a church member who got frustrated that things were not going quite as they wanted. Often in these situations, with near zero warning, the individual involved decides they are not doing this anymore and they walk out. They hurriedly stuff their promises of commitment into a bag labelled 'Me First' and head for the exit sign without giving much thought to the possible consequences of their actions and the effects they might have on others.

Of course, there are times when it is right to walk out of a situation: domestic violence, physical danger or abuse, but in everyday life, day-to-day commitment is needed to achieve good relationships so that the practical things can happen as they should. The problem I would suggest, with the people who just 'get up and go' is that they are motivated by a pivotal principle of the 'me first' factor. Romans 5:3-4 (NIV) talks about the principles of learning character. Suffering produces perseverance and this builds character. A.W. Tozer describes character as the *'excellence of moral beings'*.

A person of character has learned to endure, and to work through the challenges that life throws at them. To be big and strong enough of mind to turn down opportunities of self-gain and choose the way of self-sacrifice takes real commitment. Being a person of your word is not an easy commitment in this day and age. Working through difficulties, stopping and thinking about yourself is hard, but it will build a Godly character within you as the result of the Holy Spirit and the manifestation of Jesus in our actions. One thing we must always do in our relationships, our struggles, whatever situation we find ourselves in, is to finish them well. That shows Godly character.

Imperfect Idols

Many years ago, in my journey to becoming a Christian, a follower of Jesus Christ, I decided I would read the whole Bible front to back looking for proof of God's existence. It didn't take long before I thought I had found it. In the Old Testament there were lots of stories of people who had encountered God, and they would usually make a monument out of stone to commemorate it. Then it would say that the monument is still there to this day. It took a while before I realised that meant, 'the day the passage was written' thousands of years ago, not literally 'today'. However, I soon realised that I didn't need to travel halfway around the world for proof; there was living proof all around me in the form of people who called themselves Christians. They said they had met Jesus, that they knew God. I have to say there was something different about them. It turns out they were *living* monuments, not stone ones.

Right at the start of the Bible God says, 'Let us make human beings in our image, make them reflecting of our nature' (Genesis 1:26 MSG). Later, God commanded that humans must not make idols, or any images of God. When you join those two bits of scripture together, it makes perfect sense. If we have been made in the image of God, then we are living 'idols'. If idols started making idols, it would all be a bit silly. Our job is to be a living representation of God – not a maker of false representations of God!

Does it sound unbelievable that we mere mortals are meant to be image bearers of the loving, merciful God? If it does, I can understand why. Sadly, we are not good at representing the living God. Christians have found out that it is very hard to represent God well, because we are inclined to sin and place our modern-day idols before God.

God sent Jesus in the perfect image of his Father, God. That's why Jesus told people, 'Anyone who has seen me has seen the Father' (John 14:9 NIV). Jesus lived his life and behaved in ways that surprised many people – definitely not how they thought God was. They had created an own image of an angry or unjust God, a harsh and nasty God, but that was not how Jesus lived. Indeed, when Jesus was arrested and accused of all sorts of wrongdoings in court before the Pilate, the Roman couldn't find any proof of the charges set against Jesus. Pilate tried to create an opportunity to free Jesus. But this backfired and

Jesus was, as we know sent to be crucified. Even when Jesus was being nailed to the cross, he managed to forgive the Roman soldiers for doing it. One of the centurions watching was so amazed, he declared, 'Surely he was the Son of God!' (Matthew 27: 54 NIV).

I don't know where you are on your journey of faith. Maybe you are looking for God? Maybe you have found him? Maybe you have never asked the question 'Is there a living God?' The good news is you don't have to go halfway around the world, look closer to home. I hope one day you too will be an 'idol', a living monument to the God who made and loves you.

Rev. Keith Glover

In The Small Things

"And do not forget to do good and share with others, for with sacrifices
God is pleased"

(Hebrews 13:16 NIV).

In our office we have a huge display of pictures of all those people who have
served on our theatre teams over the years. It tracks our history and shows
those joining our organisation that others have walked this path too. I often
look at the photos, and as I review each one, some portraits bring a natural
smile to my face and a feeling of happiness, while for others I have a more
neutral reaction. Then there is my grimacing face, saved for some.

So why such a contrast? Sadly, It is easy to identify the people who bring on
the grimace because they created a legacy for all the wrong reasons. There was
an eighteen-year-old girl, who had the most beautiful pure singing voice, yet
when the going got a bit tough and things didn't quite run the way she wanted,
rather than sit down and work it through, she got up early and stuck a note
through the door saying 'Bye, I'm off'. That was the last we saw of her. Then
there was the lead actor whose own self-importance made him a nightmare to
work with because he wanted to be the 'Star' and was not a team player.

By contrast there are those people who brought rays of sunshine with them
even on cloudy days. The pragmatic kind who would cause a smile to break out
upon my face that reflects positive memories.

As I analyse my reaction, I realise that these sunshine people all shared a
common characteristic; each of them was able to think beyond their role or
their own needs. They had developed a natural radar of emotion or practical
intellect that extended beyond their own world. It was often their acts of
kindness that made them stand out: The member who made bookmarks for
everyone with words of encouragement, the person who ensured we always
had milk in the fridge. These people weren't just a part of the day to day
running of the company, their unselfish little touches, thinking beyond the
basics, were adding warmth, kindness and friendship to the troupe. The team
players were not people motived by self-interest but driven by sacrifice.

What kind of team player are you?

In Times of Trouble
(Psalm 40: 12-17)

There are times in life when everything seems hopeless, overwhelming and unsolvable. There are moments where we face unprecedented challenges when everything we have worked towards and planned for is ripped from under our feet. When we feel crippled by circumstances, battered by the waves of bad news, it can be hard to get our bearings. It is difficult to navigate a steady course to safety in the choppy sea of emotions of despair, sadness and disappointment. Who will throw us a lifebelt when we are surrounded by so many problems? What will keep us afloat? Who will rescue us when true friends seem few and far between?

Sometimes our own sin and shortcomings catch up with us, which can then become topics of conversation. Who will help when we have lost the courage to face the world and its challenges? Who will believe in the best of us in a world quick to mock and criticise? How can we feel valued when we are simply a forgotten figure? How can we discover joy and hope when we are grasping for the very breath of life itself?

In times of trouble we have so many questions and answers and it can feel quite daunting. We may ask, where is the life line of salvation when we are feeling forgotten. When waves of suffering drown out God's voice. But the presence of God is constant even when we are disorientated, disillusioned and lost in a sea of uncharted circumstance and emotions.

It is in these times that we may need to shout above the noise and simply yell! 'Please O Lord, come quickly and save me!' (Psalm 40:13 NIV)
'You are my help, and my deliverer. O God, Do not delay! ' (Psalm :17 NIV).

It isn't wrong to lament your feelings with God, to pour out your heart, to weep in anguish, to cry out: 'O God, do not delay in my time of stress'.

Prayer:
In my moment of hopelessness, in the feeling of separation and disillusionment. Come quickly Lord and fill that void. Save me.

Amen .

John Newton (1725 –1807)
Slave Trader to Priest

Amazing Grace, is a hymn written by John Newton, who penned it from personal experience. He was a man with no morals, whose life was transformed by the power of God's grace.

At the age of seven, Newton's mother, his spiritual influence, died leaving him at the mercy of his distant father. His father's profession was spent at sea. John accompanied his father on sea voyages that gave him a stern education in seamanship. He eventually parted company with his father and he was pressed (conscripted) into service with the Royal Navy, where he was little prepared for the hardships, the rough crew, and dangers on board England's floating military. Newton fell far from his mother's early spiritual influence and he became an unruly young lad with no morals. Unlicensed, he gave into his lusts and become a foul-mouthed blasphemer, engaging in gambling and drinking. He hated life in the Navy and secured a crew exchange with a merchant ship/slave trader, bound for the west African Coast.

He soon found himself well-established within the transatlantic slave trade, transporting slaves to be sold for work on the sugar plantations in the west Indies and the cash crops in Southern America.

In 1748, whilst on a voyage, the ship he was aboard encountered a severe storm off the coast of Donegal, Ireland. It was filling with water fast and was on the verge on going down. In desperation, Newton called out to God to save the ship. Though the vessel was badly damaged, they miraculously survived and limped home to Liverpool.

Even though John had called out to God in his hour of need, he soon returned to his old ways. But the seed of grace had been sown. Over the next few years, John gradually began to discover the mercy of the living God and, slowly, he developed a hunger for Christian theology. He continued to work in the slave trade; like so many others in eighteenth century society, he saw it as an honourable profession. Newton had clearly become a changed man and this started to affect him. As captain, he treated his cargo of slaves better than most captains.

In 1755, a sudden seizure whilst on shore leave, forced him to give up his seafaring days. He worked as a tide surveyor (a tax collector) in the dockyards of Liverpool for ten years and this is where he wrote his life story to share with others. He felt God's calling to become a clergyman, but the path was not easy for him as he had never received an education, and the Church of England were rather reluctant to make him a minister. Finally, the influential Earl of Dartmouth recommended Newton and he was offered a post in Olney, Buckinghamshire. There he started his ministry, supported by his wife Mary. His preaching became so popular that the church added a gallery to accommodate those who flocked to hear him. Newton was a prolific hymn writer too, one of them being *Amazing Grace*. After sixteen years, he became the rector of St Mary Woolnoth, Lombard Street, London. There, he became an ally of William Wilberforce.

Thirty-four years after he had retired from the slave trade, he published *Thoughts upon the Slave Trade*, in which he described the squalid conditions on board a slave ship. He had copies sent to every MP and the pamphlet sold so well that it was swiftly re-printed. This strengthened the case for the abolition of the slave trade.

He died on 21st December 1807 an old man whose sight had failed but he knew that the British Parliament had brought in an act of prohibiting the slave trade in the British Empire. While this did not totally stop this barbaric trade, it was an important step towards making it illegal.

John found God's Amazing Grace, a person who was lost was now found.

Amazing grace how sweet the sound
That saved a wretch like me.
I once was lost but now I'm found.
Was blind but now I see.

John Newton (1725-1807)

Judas
A Monologue

We've got a big problem with Judas. He stormed into the office telling me he changed his mind and wanted out. I told him, once you are in you are in, there's no get out clause, no tracking back, no emergency exit. He wanted to do a new deal. I told him there's no refund policy. "Didn't you read the small print?" I said to him. Then he starts pleading, bleating like a little lamb, pacing the room, berating himself. He just went on and on, I thought any minute he's was going to get on his knees and start begging. How embarrassing would that have been? He wanted to renegotiate. I told him he cannot change what was done.

I said to him, imagine you're a burglar, you break into a home, you trash the home until you find the jewel and cash, make off with the loot and exit the scene – cash in hand, job done. Then, the next day you wake up with a guilty conscious about robbery. You cannot just turn up at the owners' home telling them you had a change of heart and that house breaking isn't your thing after all. So you decided to return the possessions, apologising for your actions and offering to help with the clean-up!. You cannot pretend it never happened, there are always consequences for your actions.

Then he starts weeping, he keeps repeating 'What have I done, what have I done?'. I try to calm him down, but he is inconsolable. So I attempt to reason with him.

"Remember" I say, "you told me you were always an outsider, you were the only one not from of Galilee. They were the brotherhood you were the outsider, you were the sidekick." That seems to stun him, and he sinks despairingly into the chair and buries his head into his hands. I put my hand on his shoulder to reassure him, but he rejects it. I can see the silent tears dropping to the floor of this broken man consumed by regret: A follower who has knowingly betrayed his master.

After that he stood up and started yelling at me.
"I trusted you, I trusted you." He accused me of being a liar and manipulating the situation to protect our religious institution. Calling us 'snakes, a brood of

vipers,' and accusing us of keeping the people in spiritual darkness. I told him it was he who came to us and wanted a deal, he who had supplied the information, and he who was happy to take the money.

"Now you have to live with it" I told him. Do I care?

For a moment he seemed tongue-tied, unable to collect his thoughts or form his words. Then he pulled out his wallet to make a payment. With his low voice barely audible, he counted out the notes, one to thirty. Placing thirty notes on the table between us he said,

"Please, take the dosh back, I don't want it. You have to release Jesus, I made a terrible mistake. I have sinned and betrayed an innocent man. Please help." I told him the deal was closed and there would be no re-negotiations. The clock could not be turned back, that hour had passed. He must take the money leave. But he thought it would become 'blood money'. He picked it up, looked at it for a while, before angrily throwing it back at me, shouting abuse and accusations before he stormed off.

That was the last I saw of him. I just don't think he could live with his guilt, the weight of the betrayal and the emotional torture. He knew he would be a marked man for the rest of his life. He was a man who wanted to either turn back the clock or find forgiveness. He got neither.

This story is told in the New International Version of the Bible in the following places:
Matthew 26:14-16, Matthew 26:47-51, Matthew 27:3-10

Let Us Not Forget

The coronavirus pandemic forced us to see things in a different light, and caused us to realise how fragile our way of life actually was. No one was immune from the life-threatening virus. Initially there was no vaccine, just an infection that would overwhelm the immune system and thousands would die before their time. As the virus spread across the nations, countries shut up shop. In the UK we were told to 'Stay at home, protect the NHS and save lives'. With firms facing the abyss of insolvency, the government launched a furlough scheme to pay eighty percent of peoples' wages if they were unable to work. An intervention that would cost over one hundred billion pounds. We all hoped our combined effects would stop the reinfection (reduce the 'R' rate as it was known).

In lockdown, the sense of all that was 'normal' had been ripped away and replaced by imposed confinement within the four walls of our homes or, if you were lucky, a home with a garden. There was little traffic, aeroplanes were grounded and the world became an eerily quiet place, where birdsong replaced the buzz of mechanical sounds. With the world grinding to a halt and the death toll rising, we refocused our values on those serving the community; those who were fighting to save lives, key workers keeping our society going. Thursday night became a time to 'clap for key workers', a recognition of those who had been heroes for the nation when for years they had gone without recognition of their true contribution to our way of life.

The story of hospital porter Mike Brown (61) sums it up. For over twenty years he had been transporting sick patients around Southampton Hospital. His job was at the lower end of the pay scale. Sadly, he contracted coronavirus and even ventilation treatment in the critical care unit failed to save his life. When his cortège drove past Southampton Hospital, hundreds of colleagues came out and paid their respects and clapped as his coffin passed. Suddenly, the role he had played was recognised as valuable to the hospital; a person who had served us without recognition for years was elevated as a true example of servanthood. It was as the Bible verse in Mark 9: 35 NIV says,

"Anyone who wants to be first must be the very last, and the servant of all."

Life to the Full

"I am the gate; whoever enters through me will be saved. They will come in and go out, and find pasture. The thief comes only to steal and kill and destroy; I have come that they may have life, and have it to the full. I am the good shepherd. The good shepherd lays down his life for the sheep"

(John 10: 9-11 NIV).

As a child I used to enjoy watching a cartoon about a super earthworm, whose catchphrase was, 'Here I come to save the day'. I adopted this for myself and took great delight in embarrassing my family by singing it at full volume in public whenever it seemed fitting. Alas, although I might be able to: help lift a heavy object, buy lunch, or even mend something that is broken, the reality is, the extent of my 'saving the day' abilities are usually rather limited.

There are those who try to 'save the day' on a larger stage too. Whilst some are well meaning and undeniably do a great deal of good, there are others whose voices sound benevolent, but who are certainly not saving the day. That's who these thieves are in v10; false teachers, who don't proclaim God's truth, but instead, their own thoughts. With fine sounding words they may appear to be saying what our messed-up world needs and wants to hear. Yet, ultimately, if it is not based on God's truth it will prove not just inadequate, but deadly.

However, there is one whose voice can be trusted; one who speaks the truth and knows what's best for us, even when it's not popular or easy to hear. One who loves his sheep so much that he lays down his life for them. He is not 'all mouth, no action', he is not all out for what he can get from us — be that money, 'likes', or votes. He truly wants to give us what is best. He is the Good Shepherd, who loves us with an uncompromising, genuine love. He doesn't want to just 'save the day', but to save us and remake us fit for eternity. He is the one we can entrust ourselves to. In him, we have someone worth living for; a future worth living for, a Saviour worth living for. So, who will you listen to today? The Good Shepherd comes to give you life to the full. So, let me urge you to listen to his voice, because only he can really 'save the day'.

Matthew Neal

Loneliness

I wonder what image the word 'Loneliness' brings to your mind? To me, it conjures up a picture of an old man sitting next to a one-bar electric heater. I glance around his room; the picture I get reveals dust on the sideboard, poor décor and a sepia wedding photograph of his late wife. My image is a poor portrait, as loneliness can affect people of any age, whether married or single. In fact, I believe most people have experienced the pain of loneliness at some stage. It is a feeling inside you, a state of being, a sense of loss. It is a lack of direction. It is discouragement. It is being misunderstood. It is having no one to talk to about everyday things. It is a sense of being unworthy, of feeling neglected. Loneliness can be with us for a fleeting moment or for a long period of time.

Each of us experience moments of loneliness. I remember an occasion: when I suddenly felt it: We had been booked to perform one of our drama shows during the Christmas season. At the end of the show, we packed everything up and that was that. Afterwards, I wanted to go for a Christmas drink, wind down and chat about it, but everyone was in a rush, some to seasonal parties. Basically, no one wanted to drive to the drama store and unload the equipment, especially on a cold winter night, so having no social engagements, I was left with the job.

I arrived at the storage shed that was located in someone's large garden and started the difficult task of transferring the cumbersome equipment from van to store. This was not an easy job as it involved struggling with heavy equipment down a long path, and negotiating several gates, which refused to jam open. Back and forth I went, the weight was tiring. For a moment, I stopped to catch my breath and at that moment it hit me, that in this struggle I felt alone – very alone. It was compounded by the fact that the drama store was behind someone's house and from the path I could see a couple watching TV in front of a glowing coal fire. It looked so cosy, so complete, compared to the chilly night I was enduring. I felt so alone, so detached from their secure world.

This was just a moment of loneliness. it was fleeting. However, for some, loneliness lasts for weeks, months and sadly even years. It is not confined to a particular gender or stage of life.

A survey completed by The Mental Health Foundation highlighted an epidemic of loneliness amongst young people between the ages of 18- 34. One in four men who call the Samaritans mention loneliness or isolation. However, the National Health Service also concluded that more than a million older people go without speaking to a friend, neighbour or family member for at least a month. Social isolation is the norm for so many as age increases. Retiring from the workplace, the deaths of spouses and friends, disability or illness can all result in loss of identity and feeling valued. These factors can all contribute to isolation, vulnerability and long-term loneliness.

It would be so easy to just stick a Bible verse on the end of this piece like a temporary sticking plaster and say 'There is your answer'. But loneliness is a complicated issue that is common to humankind at every life stage. My hope is that by highlighting and raising awareness of the issue, it may help you recognise that you are not alone in times of loneliness, and that others feel the same.

If this resonates with you, then maybe recognition can be the first step towards reconnection.

Methodism: The John Wesley Story
(1703 -1791)

Being the fifteenth child of the Rector of Epworth was not easy, it literally meant that as soon as you could talk, a large section of scripture had to be memorized. John Wesley was no exception to this and his childhood experiences were full of adversity. At the age of five the family home caught fire, trapping John on the upper floor. He was saved by a parishioner standing on another man's shoulders who managed to drag him out through a window. Throughout his childhood standards were set, and he was expected to become proficient in both Latin and Greek. As he grew older his studies continued at Oxford, where eventually, John was ordained as an Anglican priest. There he stayed and became a tutor and Fellow of Lincoln College. His brother Charles, and like-minded friends at the same university formed a so-called 'Holy Club', which John joined. He eventually became the leader and introduced methods that comprised of a list of questions that one could use to review and challenge one's soul. They were mocked by fellow students who nick-named them the Methodists.

At thirty-two John grew weary of being a 'Fellow' and in 1735 sailed to the new British colony of Georgia to fulfil the vacancy of Clergyman. The North American outpost had been established two years previously when debtors were given the option of making up this new colony instead of languishing in prison. John intended to take the gospel to the native savages and pastor the flock. On his voyage he encountered both raging storms and Moravian Christians. The latter challenged his understanding of faith.

In his new parish, he quickly alienated swathes of the community with his heavy-handed approach and legalism. Matters got worse for him when he considered marrying a woman called Sophia. Not knowing what to do, he drew lots to help him decide. The result was, he was not to marry. However, he longed for her company and when she married someone else it became a stumbling block to him. Tensions escalated and the whole community became involved when he refused to give communion to the newly married couple. The uproar became so intense that John fled and boarded a ship for England under the cover of darkness. Broken and distraught, he subsided into depression.

During John's two-year absence, fellow members of the 'Holy Club' had taken up posts across England. Thus, sprung up a handful of Holy (Methodist) groups.

Another encounter with a Moravian Christian then challenged John's perception of how one must be saved. Slowly he accepted that it was by faith and grace that people are saved, rather than good works purifying the soul, a person was transformed from the inside out. He set about telling others his new theology. However, he met strong opposition and offended many people, so much so, that he was banned form preaching in all London churches, in fact in the end he was only allowed to speak in four churches in England.

In 1739, George Whitefield invited John to Bristol to witness his open-air preaching to which thousands of crude and uneducated miners came. However, soon after John's arrival Whitefield announced that he was off to Georgia. This left the outreach work to John.

Though lacking experience, he preached to up to fifteen thousand people daily who had never set foot in a church. At these gatherings some strange things began to happen as God began to touch people by his Holy Spirit. Some people started shrieking, others laughed hilariously or spoke in other tongues, whilst others trembled and fell to the ground. Understandably, this drew much criticism from the Church of England.

Around this time, John also let another love interest slip through his fingers, and when he did marry it was not the soul mate he had hoped for. They eventually separated.

However, the momentum continued, small pastoral groups were formed, and a building followed. John encouraged lay preachers' involvement which was also frowned upon by the Church of England. As Methodism grew across the country and around the world, persecution became a way of life for the flock. When he went to preach, church bells would be rung to drown him out. In his fifty years preaching it is estimated he travelled two hundred and fifty thousand miles on horseback. At the age of seventy-nine he would rise at 4am ready to share the gospel.

Today there are 75 million people worldwide who call themselves 'Methodists'.

Misadventures

I seem to have been blessed with an uncanny ability to get myself into embarrassing situations. On one occasion quite recently, I managed to lean back, like Derek Trotter in *Only Fools and Horses*, and fall backwards into a cupboard. Later that day as I waited in the playground to pick up my kids from school, I was playing with a water pistol I happened to have in my pocket (as you do). One misdirected tweak of the trigger and there I was, in full view of all the mums, with a disconcerting wet patch on the front of my trousers. Then, when I got home, I walked straight into the patio door. You see, however much I like to see myself as Mr Cool, sadly the evidence suggests otherwise.

In all the time I've known God, I've heard him talk to me in many different ways. He speaks to me through his word, through conversations with friends, through speakers at church and at other events, through the places I've travelled to and the experiences I've had – even through the untimely mishaps of my daily routines, and he speaks straight to my heart.

Through both the good times and the bad, I've been constantly aware of God's voice. I've watched him at work in my life, and he's taught me some valuable lessons. Some of these have been learned the hard way, through struggle and heartache, others through sheer, out and out slogging away.

But throughout my embarrassments, struggles and misadventures, I've always been up for God speaking to me through them. It really is the best way to be.

Steve Legg

My Travelling Companion

"Religion that God our father accepts as pure and faultless is this: To look after orphans and widows in their distress and to keep oneself from being polluted by the world"

(James 1:27 NIV).

Years ago, when I drove to work, I had a little routine: at 7.00am I would turn on the radio and listen to Radio 4. On this occasion the broadcaster's voice came across unusually hesitant and slightly emotional. There was a pause, then he announced in a solemn tone. 'I am sad to tell you Brian Redwood has died'. I felt a wave of sadness envelop me. Brian had been my friend, my morning travelling companion for over ten years as I commuted on the traffic-laden M3 motorway.

For most of you, Brian Redwood will be an unknown name. Yet for myself and seven million other listeners at the time, he was the voice that brought current affairs and world events into our lives as we started our day. Sadly, Brian and I had completed our final car journey together. I felt sorrow for a man I had never met, Brian had been my invisible car companion and I knew I would miss him.

Today, someone will be losing not an invisible friend, but their soul mate, a close family member, or a lifetime companion.

Over the years I have encountered many people whose spouses have left the world prematurely, often at the hand of cancer. Their pain is still palpable as they struggle to come to terms with such loss. I have often struggled to find words of comfort to say to a widow, who for the first time in years, is facing a world of being single. I have to be honest, I try not to say too much, partly out of fear of passing a trivial comment that is more damaging than helpful as know I will not fully understand their situation. Usually, the only support I can offer is a few minutes of listening. I hope that God uses those few moments somehow.

The Bible talks about caring for widows. Let us try hard not to be too busy or fearful to ask a person who has suffered bereavement, how they are. We need to be aware that loss is not short-term pain but a lingering sorrow, and that their world is a quieter place without their travelling companion.

Nehemiah - An Introduction to The Story in Historic Content

During the time of *The Assyrian Empire* (1100 - 625 BC), the northern kingdom of Israel had been defeated and all its inhabitants carried away into captivity, (721 BC). Most of the southern kingdom of Judah was now under the control of the Assyrian army. However, God protected the Holy city of Jerusalem and its Solomon temple.

The Babylonians sent the Assyrians packing and became the dominant empire from 625-536 BC. King Nebuchadnezzar appointed Zedekiah to be king over the land of Judah and Jerusalem. Sadly, he did evil in the eyes of the Lord when he rebelled against king Nebuchadnezzar over a dispute about tribute money (tax) and entered an alliance with Egypt. This angered Nebuchadnezzar and he sent his mighty forces to besiege the city of Jerusalem. After two years of blockade the starving occupants of the city finally succumbed to the Babylonians. The conquering army then ransacked the city and the Holy Temple and burnt everything in sight. Most of the Jews were then deported to the city of Babylon.

Forty-eight years later (536 BC) King Cyrus the Persian King conquered the Babylonians and became the dominant power in the region. The surviving Jews were still in captivity, but the Persians had a relaxed attitude towards a multifaith culture and allowed the Jews to practice their religion. Some were even granted permission to return to the holy city of Jerusalem. A second wave of Jews followed under the leadership of Ezra (458 BC). They rebuilt the temple but not the defence walls or the gates of the city. This left them exposed to attack.

Nehemiah's story begins in 445 BC:

Nehemiah entered after the second re-population of Jerusalem with the city defence still in a state of disrepair. Nehemiah was a trusted official in the ancient courts and the cupbearer to King Artaxerxes. Basically, his job description was to taste the wine and check it hadn't been poisoned before the King drunk it. This could have been a dead-end job...literally. While working for the King, Nehemiah heard of the terrible plight and distress of the Jews living in city with broken walls and gates. His distress was so great that he sat down and wept, fasted and prayed to God. Later, he asked the king for permission to return and rebuild the city. He was so persuasive that he gained letters expressing the king's support for the venture, and permits for building material such as timber from the King's forest. Upon arrival in Jerusalem, at night time under the cover of darkness he secretly inspected the damaged walls and then organised the people so that reconstruction of the city walls and gates could begin. When rebuilding, the workers faced outside opposition, so they worked with their tools in one hand and a sword in the other. Each brick laid was a step forward in the battle to restore the protective walls of the city. Nehemiah also had to resolve an internal problem as rich Jews were profiting from poor countrymen. Nehemiah had to stop the racketeering and restore justice.

Through good management and prayer, astonishingly, fifty-two days later, the project was completed. It was a momentous achievement and sent out the message that the God of Israel was with these people. It is a story of a godly a man willing to step into the gap and make the difference. The story continues with the people recommitted to worshiping the God of Israel.

Nehemiah: A Man of Prayer

"When I heard these things, I sat down and wept. For some days I mourned and fasted and prayed before the God of heaven"

(Nehemiah 1:4 NIV).

Nehemiah had heard that God's people who had returned from exile to Jerusalem were living in dire straits; the walls of their city had been broken down and the gates burned. Nehemiah's response gives us a blueprint for effective intercession, he identified the need and became emotionally involved, seeking God in prayer.

In our busy lives, we should be aware of the needs of those around us, keep ourselves informed of current events and not bury our heads in the sand. We need to be willing to be moved to pray and act, to feel God's heart and pain. Maybe next time you watch the news and hear of a specific situation, instead of feeling helpless and hopeless, you can ask God how He wants you to pray for those individuals involved.

Romans: 8.26 (The Passion Translation), says; 'At times we don't even know how to pray, or know the best things to ask for, but the Holy Spirit rises up within us to super-intercede on our behalf, pleading to God with emotional sighs too deep for words.'

Nehemiah heard the disturbing reports, He became an intercessor and was then spurred into action. I think that during Nehemiah's period of prayer and fasting, (reckoned to be about four months), God gave him an action plan, a strategy for rebuilding the walls. This included obtaining the King's permission; when the opportunity arose, he approached the King with fear and trepidation, the result was, he found favour with him.

Time spent in prayer will prepare us to hear God's voice and empower us to take action. How prepared are we to spend time with God in intercession for those around us, or for the world events, or to feel God's heart for others and be prepared to be the answer to our own prayers?

Marion Boyton

Nehemiah – The Encourager

"Wherever you hear the sound of the trumpet, join us there. Our God will fight for us!"

(Nehemiah 4:20 NIV).

How secure would you feel if the front door of your house had been kicked in and then ripped off its hinges? The people of Jerusalem found themselves in a more extreme situation when King Nebuchadnezzar's Babylonian army ransacked the city of Jerusalem leaving the city walls and gates in ruin.

Fast forward Forty-eight years: The Babylonians Kingdom had been dispatched by a more liberal Persian Empire. The King of Persia permits Ezra, a Jewish scribe and priest to organise two groups of Judean exiles to be released from captivity and returned home to Jerusalem to rebuild the temple and restore Jewish spirituality. Ezra achieves this but the city's defences remain in ruin.

Fast forward another ninety-one years and Nehemiah enters the scene and on learning of their plight is motivated to divinely intervene. After much prayer and fasting during his months of intercession he experiences a spiritual breakthrough with God. He is then appointed province governor of Judah with permission to rebuild the city.

Nehemiah encouraged God's people to rebuild the walls and gates of Jerusalem by speaking of God's will using words to bring life and hope. He was able to motivate them by sharing his own answer to prayer, and letting them know that God had already given him favour with the king (Nehemiah 2:18 NIV). Nehemiah helped them overcome their fear of the enemy by telling them to focus on God and his power. He gathered the people together to work as a team and support each other in rebuilding the walls and resisting the enemy, reminding them that God was with them.

Spend time with God now, asking him to help you focus on him, so that you can be an encourager and speak words of life to those around you. Words and actions that, like Nehemiah make a difference – that repair metaphorical doors, that have been ripped of their hinges.

Prayer:

Let my words help bring healing to those who carry pain.
Let my actions, not be self motivated.
May my deeds promote teamwork and community.
Help me to be a person who is willing to give up rights and ideas for the common good.
Help me be an instrument of love in a world of broken walls.

Amen.

Marion and Barry Boyton

Nehemiah – Wise Protector

"Remember the Lord, who is great and awesome, and fight for your families, your sons and your daughters, your wives and your homes"

(Nehemiah 4:13 NIV)

Nehemiah's actions caused opposition from the enemy. You can guarantee that if we begin stepping out in obedience to God, our enemy the Devil won't like it either. Nehemiah's enemies mocked and ridiculed him and his team, but he answered them confidently, saying: 'The God of heaven will give us success. We, his servants will start rebuilding, but as for you, you have no share in Jerusalem or any claim or historic right to it' (Nehemiah 2: 20 NIV).

Like Nehemiah, we can be confident in God. We can speak God's word with authority against the accusations and ridicule of our enemy. Ephesians 6:18 NIV, talks of the sword of the Spirit which is the Word of God. Jesus used this against the enemy when he was tempted in the wilderness, countering every accusation of the Devil with a quote from God's word.

We can see further parallels between Nehemiah's battle and ours. Nehemiah 4 NIV describes how Hebrews stayed alert against enemy attack, praying and setting a guard, day and night behind the builders, watching their backs. They posted armed watchmen in the exposed places and ensured that there was always someone ready to defend them. In 1 Peter 5:8-9 (NIV) it says: 'Be alert and of sober mind. Your enemy the devil prowls around like a roaring lion looking for someone to devour. Resist him, standing firm in the faith'.

We need to pray, stay vigilant and look out for one another, watching each other's backs. Let us be ready to stand against our enemy's accusations with the sword of the Spirit: the power of God's Word.

Marion Boyton

Our Resurrection Body

"The splendor of the heavenly bodies is one kind, and the splendor of the earthly bodies is another. The sun has one kind of splendor, the moon another and the stars another; and star differs from star in splendor.

(1 Cor. 15:40-41 NIV)

I have often heard old people say, 'Whatever you do, don't get old.'

The ageing process is one thing all of humanity has in common. As the minutes turn to days, the days to months, and the months to years, we grow older. You can battle against the ageing process, but you will always be on the losing side. Of course, working out at the gym, keeping the weight down, and making good lifestyle choices may extend your longevity but there is one simple fact that is inevitable – your body has been decaying since birth, and will keep on decaying. You are like a complicated car; your engine is motoring along life's highway. Youth has the mobility to accelerate to full speed, but at some stage, everyone is going to need to take the foot off the gas pedal and settle for a reasonable pace. Occasionally, a part breaks and a replacement is installed – a replacement hip, a heart bypass, etc. With a little care you can carry on for a while, however, the fact is that one day we will be beyond repair and the motor of life will grind to a halt.

The Bible promises that those who believe in Christ will have new bodies, which, as you get older, becomes more appealing. So, what will our resurrection body be like? None of us know.

We can find an example of death and resurrection in gardening. You plant a 'dead' seed and soon there is a flourishing plant. There is no visual likeness between seed and plant. You could never guess what a tomato plant would look like by looking at a tomato seed. What we plant in the soil and what grows out of it doesn't look anything alike. The dead body that we bury in the ground, and the resurrection body that comes from it will be dramatically different. One thing for certain – our new bodies will be AWESOME.

Paradoxes

The Christian life is a life of paradoxes.
We must give to receive,
realize we are blind to see,
become simple to be wise,
suffer for gain,
and die to live.

Asahel Nettleton

Asahel Nettleton *(1783 –1844) was an American theologian and Evangelist from Connecticut, USA. He was used by God to bring revival to Congregationalist churches in New England. Before preaching in any area, he would often move into a community for several months getting to know its spiritual needs. He did not believe in 'altar calls' or 'revival meetings' as he believed salvation was a work of God alone. It is estimated that thirty thousand people came to faith through his ministry. In later life his was in poor health which restricted his travel.* 2.

2. Ref: Quote, *Azquotes.com.* Description, *Wikipedia*

Parenthood

"And now these three remain: faith, hope and love. But the greatest of these is love."

(1 Corinthians 13:13 NIV).

If you haven't experienced this embarrassment personally, there is a high chance you have been a witness to it; the toddler meltdown in the middle of the supermarket, the wrestling of wills, the determination of a two-year-old who randomly wants to buy a product because they like the colour of the packaging. A battle erupts with the child's will pitched against the wisdom of their parent. The screaming child creates an unpleasant sound that draws a steady stream of curious spectators. Some shoppers cast disparaging looks, others give a sympathetic glance. Then, to elevate the stakes the toddler starts rolling on the floor, throwing arms and legs around in the motion of badly executed swim strokes; the flapping front crawl, the beating breaststroke and offbeat butterfly stroke. The child is enraged that they haven't got what they wanted, and now, everyone is knows about it. Somehow, at the age of two and a half they have discovered the art of embarrassing the parent and are becoming practised at the act of manipulation.

Choosing to become a parent is a mad thing to do. Couples embark on this journey of parenthood without reading the terms and conditions and comprehending the realities. It can be tough going; being vomited over, having to clean up poo, surviving on four hours of interrupted sleep is a high call. The effect on your marriage can be difficult too, instead of just the two of you, you become a family unit and the level of intimacy you once enjoyed can be interrupted.

On the positive side, being a parent brings times of pure joy, laughter and awe. There are wonderful rewarding moments when raising offspring. But your children will always test your resolve, patience and stamina. The sheer hard work, the financial restraints, and the late nights and even the occasional trip to the accident and emergency department swiftly confirms this for anyone in doubt. All this can take its toll on Mum and Dad. Parents at times can feel exhausted emotionally and physically. Then there are the supermarket meltdowns which put child and parent in direct conflict in a public arena with an audience of bystanders. A tired parent trying to hold their nerve when inside their head a voice is desperately shouting, 'I cannot do this anymore'.

What keeps parents going when patience and energy is depleted and fatigue has become all consuming?

It is the greatest gift of all: Love – unconditional love that finds something to give, when nothing is left.

Pay it Forward

"Do to others as you would have them do to you"

(Luke 6:31 NIV).

A few years ago, there was a movie called *Pay it Forward*. It was a film that followed a twelve-year-old called Trevor McKinney, who launches a good will movement. The central idea behind the film was similar to the Bible verse 'Do to others as you would have them do to you' (Luke 6:31). In the film, Trevor helps three people with something they can't do themselves. The recipient can't return the favour but instead must 'pay it forward' by helping three other people. The idea is, that if everyone did this, the world would be transformed and become a kinder place. It was a refreshing offering from Hollywood.

However, in reality we all know that this principle will break down at some point: A few years ago, a speaker at a youth meeting decided as part of his talk to do a kind of 'live lab test' with the young people in his company. He produced a valuable bank note and asked a youth to pass it from one person to another along the row. He would collect the money once it reached the back of the gathering. All started well and the note was passed from one person to another. However, at some stage the money disappeared and never reached the back of the hall. The temptation of the cash was just too much for someone. Thus the 'pass it on' principle had broken down.

The words of Jesus 'Do to others as you would have them do to you' are not an option but a commandment. They encapsulate God's central commandment, 'Love your neighbour as you love yourself' (Mark 12.31 NIV). It is a challenge to our selfishness. This command is the 'Law of Love', it causes us to lay down our lives for each other. It is a command that affects every area of our lives. It is not often rewarding, mostly it is about personal sacrifice rather than self-gain. It is choosing to prefer to, pay it forward, to lay down our lives for each other, just as Christ laid down his life for us.

I love this quote *(source unknown):*

'We make a living by what we get. We make a life by what we give'.

Perhaps God

"Perhaps the Lord will act on our behalf"

(1 Samuel 14: 6 NIV).

Firstly, I recommend that you read the whole story in 1 Samuel 14: 1-14 to gain an overview of the situation. You will see that the Israelites were in a pretty bad situation. Their army was scattering – scared of the Philistines around them and lacking weapons. What is more, their king, Saul, has disobeyed God and has just been told that someone else will take over the kingdom. It all seems hopeless.

However, in the midst of all this, we find a story of faith and determination. Jonathan, Saul's son, is not content to sit around and be defeated – he wants to make a difference! He still wants to see Israel victorious and believes it is possible. Why? His faith in God's ability is clear. In verse 6 he says, 'Nothing can hinder The Lord from saving, whether by many or by few.' Whilst the rest of the Israelite army are looking at the Philistines and feeling small and outnumbered, Jonathan is looking to God, who is bigger than his enemies, and he believes that God can save Israel, even through using just two men.

Jonathan takes a step of faith, saying 'Perhaps God will act on our behalf' (1 Samuel 14: 6). God hasn't told Jonathan to go, nor promised him the defeat of the Philistines, but Jonathan's attitude is not one of waiting around for a calling. He may not be sure that God will act, but he is confident God is able to. He is willing to take the risk to serve God and save his people.

I wonder whether we could have more of a 'Perhaps God' attitude? Through the Bible, God shows us his heart and how he wants us to live, and I believe this means we can act on his will without needing a specific calling or instruction for everything we do.

There are times when waiting on God is definitely a good thing, but we won't always have a voice from heaven telling us what to do. We need to try proactively living out what God has taught us, trusting that He will correct us where we go wrong, and praying that 'perhaps God' will help us in ways we can't even imagine. Staying still, waiting for instruction, isn't always the best way to receive direction.

'You cannot travel in a parked car'. There is no need for a Sat Nav if you are stationary, Let's start the journey.

Adapted by *Joanna Hodgson* based on sermon preached by *Phil Marsden.*

Perseverance

"Consider it pure joy, my brothers and sisters, whenever you face trials of many kinds, because you know that the testing of your faith produces perseverance"

(James 1:2-3 NIV).

James Dyson, the inventor and manufacturing entrepreneur, always had a love for design. Probably best known for inventing the bagless vacuum cleaner, his journey to success was not an easy one. Years earlier, he invented the ball barrow – a wheelbarrow with a ball instead of a wheel to eliminate punctures and prevent it from getting stuck in small holes. His prototype wasn't met with enthusiasm by the manufacturers, but he persisted and soon overcame the problems. After very little interest from garden centres, he put a simple advert in the newspaper and the orders came flooding in. Sadly, ripped off by an employee, his association with the invention was short-lived. Losing a court battle, he was ousted from the board and lost the rights to his invention.

His rocky road to success didn't stop there. Along with cash flow problems, he spent years travelling around Europe, America and Japan trying to get his vacuum cleaner project off the ground. He had built over five thousand prototypes before it was accepted by the manufacturers. With fourteen years between idea and production line, the financial and physical toll was high ... but success finally came. Now a household name around the world, James Dyson is a truly remarkable example of someone with dogged determination.

The Bible says that as Christians, we too will face trials of many kinds. Do we have something to learn from Dyson's perseverance when we're faced with suffering and up-hill struggles? When our own business looks like it's failing? When we feel all alone? When we've lost money, friends, or relationships with family members? When we feel like throwing in the towel on our Christian beliefs? Perseverance isn't an attribute you are born with, it is something we learn hour by hour, day by day, month by month. It is hoping and believing that the future will be better than the past. It is embarking on a creative journey where we can overcome the near impossible when we need to, making progress one step at a time.

Pew Rental

"I thank my God ... because of your partnership in the gospel"

(Philippians 1:3,5 NIV).

Attending church services can become something we just take for granted that we will always be able to do. Church services and associated activities don't just happen. Many of us are blissfully unaware that behind the scenes of every church or Christian organisation there is a small mountain of expenditure; the regular bills of maintenance, direct debits for gas, water, electric, plus, the minister's wages, outlay for the administration are all costs that need to be met.

In the eighteenth century, one way they raised additional funds was by a scheme called 'pew-renting', this meant, for a payment you could rent a pew to listen to the sermon. This practise became widespread among the Anglican, Methodist and Presbyterian church. Pew renting was even given legal standing as fund raiser. However, not all was well with this 'money for a seat' scheme. It meant the wealthy could be exclusive and commandeer a pew for every member of their family, while the less fortunate were relegated to free seats which often only accounted for twenty percent of pews available. This created inequality within the House of God. Eventually protests sprung up against this practise and it was slowly withdrawn. It finally died out in the 1930s

While pew rental created disparity, it served a purpose at the time, helping to maintain many parish churches that exist today. Today we can rightfully enter a church and worship God at no personal cost, but behind the scenes the bills still roll in.

Today we are asked to be in partnership in the gospel, to support the vision and stand together as a body of believers and financially underwrite the agenda. We should do this not out of a sense of duty, but be motivated by our love for God and his church. Today, you cannot 'rent a pew', but you can choose to set up a regular donation that helps advance Gods' work at your church.

Today, I challenge you: Give generously. Give regularly to the work of God. Give to your church out of love for the kingdom of God. Set aside money for that missionary organisation that reaches those you cannot. Don't just 'sit comfortable' on the subject of giving.

Pick the Right Fight

"Then you will understand what is right and just and fair – every good
path. For wisdom will enter your heart, and knowledge will be
pleasant to your soul. Discretion will protect you, and understanding
will guard you"

(Proverbs 2: 9-11 NIV).

The following is a true story. There were once three people sharing a three-bedroom house. They had jointly signed a rental agreement with terms and conditions. It all looked good on paper. They soon discovered they were not natural friends and lived acrimoniously for the duration of a year. Nearing the expiry of the tenancy agreement the landlord inspection took place. The verdict was mainly good, a bit of expected normal 'wear and tear' and some minor chargeable damage. The bill was dispatched, the cost split equally. Two saw it as fair, but the third profoundly disagreed; he didn't want to pay. He looked up his tenancy agreement, reading every clause. He scoured the Internet to support his case. Then, composing a letter to the landlord, he presented his case – why he should not pay. The landlord wasn't impressed and stood his ground to the tenant's fury. The tenant stomped around, raving, complaining, moaning and eventually huffed and puffed all the way to the Citizen's Advice Bureau. For him, the battle had to go on, he had to prove his point and he wasn't going to pay a penny. Surrender wasn't an option in his mind. So, he persisted in fighting the landlord with an exchange of emails. All this for the grand total of twenty-two pounds.

I challenged the tenant. Is it worth the fight? Is it worth the stress? Is it worth the money? Is it worth the time? His response surprised me; he was determined to fight as in his eyes an injustice had been done.

One of the hard things to do in life is to 'pick the right fight' and walk away from the minor discrepancies. In churches, there are disagreements over music, the position of the lectern and, yes, I even heard of a nice little battle over the serving of a trifle. Christians have not always filled their boats with glory, but the real issue is that while we are consumed by the small discrepancies, we are distracted from focusing our energy on the big fights – the ones that really matter. What's the point in winning the argument if it breaks a relationship? Sometimes, we need to lay low and let the bullets go over our head. Only fight the right battles.

Prayer:
Lord, today help me to be wise in the battles I face. Give me wisdom to let go of things that have insignificance and fight for the things that have lasting eternal value. Make me a wise and discerning person. Help me to pick the right fight, at the right time.

Amen.

Praying for Our Leaders

Being a minister, pastor or church leader is never easy. The modern-day position fulfils a role that is somewhere between managing director and therapist. This is combined with a workload that demands six days a week plus, where the church flock often come before family.

It can be a role in which everyone wants a piece of them, but then few are fully satisfied with their portion.

I love the quote below from John Newton (writer of the hymn *Amazing Grace*).

You know the common expression, 'A Jack of all Trades'. I am sure a minister needs to be one as such:

> A brave soldier,
> An alert watchman,
> A caring shepherd,
> A hardworking farmer,
> A skillful builder,
> A wise counsellor,
> A competent physician and a loving nurse.

Prayer:
Lord I pray for the leaders of my church. I pray firstly that they will be people who know you, who walk daily with you and who know your will. I pray for their physical, spiritual and mental health. I pray their families find quality time together. I pray that you will give them wisdom, stamina, kindness and the ability to inspire and to deliver the correct words at the right time. I pray that they will be able to discern your vision amongst the secret agendas and the bombardment of ideas.
I pray that they will be a person of God.
Amen.

Preacher, Pastor
The DL Moody Story (1837 – 1899)

One of the greatest evangelists of our time, Dwight Moody was the seventh child of nine. After his father's death the family barely survived. At times there wasn't even enough firewood to heat their home. At the age of seventeen Moody moved to Boston and worked at his uncle's shoe shop as a salesman. Employment came on the condition that he would attend church regularly. He excelled as a salesman but was also full of mischief and had a terrible habit of swearing. Despite his rough edges, his Sunday School teacher invested time in him and led him to Christ. It was a watershed moment for Dwight.

At nineteen he moved to Chicago and found even greater success selling shoes. He attended a small church with a Sunday School. He noticed that the helpers were demoralised due to the lack of children attending. Offering to help, he wandered the neighbourhood recruiting children to attend the Sunday school. Within a week the Sunday school had grown by eighteen. Every week, the pattern was repeated. The growth in attendance led to several changes of premises to eventually accommodate 500 to 600 street children. It became the largest Sunday School in the USA. Evening services were introduced and over 1500 attended. Moody's methods of drawing people to Christ were un-conventional; they included buying a pony to attract children to church, taking baskets of food to poor houses and telling the impoverished about Jesus. He gave up shoe selling and devoted himself to Christian ministry. During the American Civil War Moody preached to thousands on both sides of the conflict.

He was also blessed with a wife, Emma. She supported in his ministry. However, Emma suffered severe asthma and on the advice of a doctor, who had suggested a trip abroad might improve her heath, they sailed to England in 1872. Moody seized the opportunity to expand the boundaries of his ministry. Unknown initially in England, he travelled the country preaching and drawing ever increasing crowds. He had arrived in England a complete unknown and left widely admired.

Back in the USA, Moody teamed up with Ira Sankey. She would write the songs and lead the singing while Moody would preach.

The great Chicago fire made over 100,000 people homeless and consumed Moody's family home. In the aftermath of the fire, Moody toured towns and cities, preaching and raising funds to help families who had lost everything. At one event he became a victim of his own success, arriving late he could not get in the building due to the vast crowds. Improvising, he clambered onto his horse-drawn carriage and started to deliver his message. Soon the coach box was surrounded.

Dwight and his family returned to England for several long missions. His loved ones would stay in London while Moody travelled from place to place, preaching. On one campaign lasting eight days, over 100,000 people came to hear him speak.

His unconventional preaching made the gospel message understandable for the common man. Moody mixed personal testimony and Bible passages. He generated so much Christian interest, that he caused a surge for copies of the Bible. However, Moody had his critics, some said he talked too fast, and used too many personal stories in preaching style.

Whether holding four-month campaigns in London or speaking in over 100 cities in the USA, thousands would come to hear this ex-shoe salesman share the Christian message of salvation. After his death, aged sixty-two, the New York Times hailed him as 'a man who did more to convert people to the Christian faith than anyone of his time'.

Prejudice

"You, therefore, have no excuse, you who pass judgment on someone else, for at whatever point you judge another, you are condemning yourself, because you who pass judgment do the same things"

(Romans 2:1 NIV).

Because I do some outreach work in prisons, a friend of mine was keen on getting myself and his friend, who found Christ in prison, together for a chat. However, the way he introduced his friend disturbed me ... he said, 'He is a nice lad, but has spent a lot time in prison, he was a rapist.' The prominent word I heard in his description was the word 'rapist'

Rape is a terrible and violating crime that wrecks people lives and the trauma it causes can have long-lasting effects on its victims. Sexual violence against women I find totally disturbing and repulsive. The crime is rightly severely punishable under law.

The description of his friend as a 'rapist' instantly built up an invisible barrier between us before we had even met face to face. When I did meet him I found it hard to fully engage because of my knowledge of his past crimes. He had found Christ, but I struggled to accept him and wondered if a person could really be that transformed. The problem was he was a labelled man. I wondered after our meeting, if he had not been tarnished by his friend's label, would I have reacted to him differently and been less guarded?

This is an extreme case, but the principle of labelling people can create a negative barrier to a friendship. How often have you given a disapproving lowdown on a person? How often have we judged someone from the background talk we have heard about them? Have we built up a prejudice on third party hearsay or part knowledge of a person's history? How can a person have a new start with Christ when we tag them with the past and label them in accordance with our own pre-judgment?

Prayer:
Lord, I pray that my view of people will not be distorted by unfair comments or preconceptions. I pray that my dealings with people will be fair, just and righteous.

Amen.

Prodigy

"It is for freedom that Christ has set us free. Stand firm, then, and do not let yourselves be burdened again by a yoke of slavery"

(Galatians 5:1 NIV).

Harry was a talented young pianist. He could play in any style and from any score. From *Beethoven* to *Queen*, he would mesmorise everybody with his skill and repertoire. Having grown tired of playing to the same old audiences in his small and sleepy hometown, he packed his bags and headed for the bright lights of London.

Harry found the music scene incredible. So many amazing venues. He could play every night – and day if he wanted to. He was making a living, a good one at that, and this was just the start. In London, everything was just so exciting. His new friends were wild, and he loved it. The girls were falling over themselves just to get near to him and doing drugs was just the norm. Harry's christian upbringing was much too boring for this; too irrelevant. He went all-in for a new life of sex, drugs and rock and roll, and it was euphoric... for a time. Then he missed a gig... then another. He used girls, and girls used him. Drugs consumed him. Before long, his passion for music was swept away by his craving for a fix. A constant, pounding craving. His life descended into two parallel worlds, one where he was trying to break free from the shackles of narcotics, and the other where he submitted to their power.

His craving was to become his death sentence when a few years later he would inject himself with heroin in a toilet in Exeter. The substance caused such a reaction that he collapsed in the cubicle. A member of the public saw his arm protruding under the toilet door and called 999. He was pronounced dead at the scene. At his funeral people said, 'What a waste of a young talented life.'

Our own life stories may not be as dramatic as Harry's, but if we've not been set free by Christ and become his slave, then we're slaves to something else. That perfect photo for Instagram, the sexy You Tube clip to wind down at the end of a tough day, or just one more drink to fill that void after a break-up; whatever might fill a hole for a moment will lead us down the dark road to spiritual death if we're not trusting in Christ for our freedom. We need rescuing from our sins, and only Christ has the power to wash us clean and set us free. We can't do it ourselves, but the one who made all things and died in our place can. Let's ask for his forgiveness and help, to set us free for a life of joyful service to him.

Prayer:

Jesus, I need you in my life, forgive my mistakes, set me free from the things that entrap me, things that dictate the direction of my life and set me heading on the wrong road. Help me not to become addicted to cravings that will consume my focus and time and enslave me.

Holy spirit come into my life afresh, create in me the strength to resist pressures from my peers. Be my counsellor in times of temptation. In a time when self-gain is the norm at other's expense.

God the Father, implant in my soul your love, your joy, your peace and righteousness.

Father, Son and Holy Spirit, may we walk side by side and have fun on the journey together.

Come into my life anew. I recommit my life to you today.

Amen.

Pruning

"I am the true vine, and my Father is the gardener. He cuts off every branch in me that bears no fruit, while every branch that does bear fruit he prunes so that it will be even more fruitful"

(John 15:1-2 NIV).

My garage office at the end of garden overlooks our solitary apple tree. It's my ever-changing companion throughout the year. I witness it bud, flower, produce fruit and then finally shed its leaves as autumn closes. Though the tree itself is dormant in the winter months I can still enjoy it and the stored apples make delicious apple crumble on cold winter nights.

To get good fruit the tree must be pruned each year. This involves giving the tree a good back and sides cut with shears. If I don't do this in the winter the following spring the tree will bear poor quality fruit. The process of pruning is essential, by removing older branches it encourages the tree to put energy into new growth as it awakens from its winter sleep.

In our Christian walk we will experience times of real growth, a closeness to God that bears fruit which can then impact upon others. Every activity we do, every church meeting we attend, every outpouring of ministering to others takes energy and commitment. My apple tree, if it was left un-pruned, would become a sprawling mess of branches, overstretched by its own growth leaving its energy supply insufficient.

My question to you is: are you overstretching yourself? Is it time to get the diary out and start cutting back? Reducing our commitments may feel like having a short back and sides, but if we don't stop occasionally and review our commitments we will simply become overstretched – burnt out, and our lives will bear little spiritual fruit. Jesus didn't say 'I have come that you may have committees, festivals and church meetings, and behold your diary will be full.' He actually said 'I have come that they may have life, and have it to the full' (John 10:10 NIV).

Prayer:
Lord, show me areas in my life where I am overstretched. Take away the unnecessary distractions that fill my time. Help me to use my skills, talents and energy well for you. Help me prune the branches of my tree that bear little fruit and to be the person who is productive, not exhausted.
Amen.

Putting Prayer First

"Very early in the morning, while it was still dark, Jesus got up, left the house and went off to a solitary place, where he prayed"

(Mark 1:35 NIV).

I want you to think about your routine. What do you prioritise? What are the most important parts of your day? What do you look forward to the most? What do you depend on the most? If we don't get our rhythm and our routine right, then we can spend major amounts of time on the minor things which only leaves us with minor amounts of time to spend on the major things. Priorities are key!

Now it's all fair and well me saying 'put the important things first', but how do we practically do this? Looking specifically at my topic for today – how do we make prayer a priority? I heard once that Martin Luther's barber asked him, 'How do you pray?' Luther explained, 'A good barber must have his thoughts, mind and eyes concentrated upon the razor and the beard and not forget where he is in his stroke and shave. If he keeps talking or thinking of something else, he is likely to cut a man's mouth or nose – or even his throat. So, anything that is to be done well ought to occupy the whole man. How much more must prayer possess the heart exclusively and completely if it is to be good prayer.'

So, what can we take from this? For me, it's that we must make a conscious decision to put prayer first and focus solely on it. We're not going to make prayer a priority if we don't choose to make it more important than anything else we have to do that day. Establishing the importance of prayer is a conscious decision to make it our priority, every day. The more we work at integrating prayer into our lives and our routines, the more in sync we are with God's plan and his direction in our life. Our day may not always go to plan, but I've definitely found that prayer makes a difference! And the more you work at putting prayer first, the more it becomes a habit, and once you've developed that habit, it cements itself as a part of your routine – your rhythm of life.

By Emma Handcock

Quietness Amongst All the Noise

"Yet the news about him spread all the more, so that crowds of people came to hear him and to be healed of their sicknesses. But Jesus often withdrew to lonely places and prayed"

(Luke 5:15,16 NIV).

Have you ever noticed how noisy and busy church can be? Even before a service starts, it's hectic. There are people testing sound levels, running the audio-visuals, and double checking the running order of the worship songs. The refreshment team are filling urns and arranging cups. The front of house 'welcomers' are chatting and organising the notice sheets. The speaker is pacing the stage, quietly practising his sermon. It is a beehive of activity, all working towards a deadline. Then the congregation start to enter. Some families with young children arrive in a state of trauma after the ordeal of getting the children up and dressed, out the door, into the car and to the building. Other members turn up late with bedraggled nocturnal teenagers who had simply refused to acknowledge that nine O'clock in the morning is a reasonable hour to get ready for church and insisting that English is best spoken in a series of inaudible grunts. Combine all this with the general background noise of other people greeting each other and the decibels increase rapidly. Then, the church service commences and the orderly arrangement of worship, prayer and preaching flows.

At the end of the service, when the final prayer is done and dusted, it is as though someone blows a whistle for kick off. Suddenly, there is an explosion of activity. This frantic time is called 'having fellowship'.

Church is important for worship, teaching and sharing life, but your relationship with God is not dependent on your church attendance. At times in our busy lives it may be good to avoid the crowd, to stop and find that comfortable resting space and meet with God by yourself – Just you and God reconnecting through personal prayer or study. It is from a place of rest that we find God's strength. We need to know God so that we can make him known to others.

Do you have a quiet place to meet with God?

Read All About It!

"Do not let any unwholesome talk come out of your mouths, but only what is helpful for building others up according to their needs, that it may benefit those who listen"

(Ephesians 4:29 NIV).

A college lecturer held up two newspaper reports side by side. They had both reported on a crown court case, where a verdict of guilty of murder had been given for an individual. Both newspapers had a photograph of the man. One newspaper contained the headline 'Found Guilty'. The other newspaper had 'Guilty' as its headline. The lecturer simply asked his students which newspaper was reporting fact and which was expressing an opinion. We may say that it is irrelevant whether the man was 'found guilty' or just 'guilty' because either way he received his sentence for the crime. However, there is a difference – being 'found guilty' indicates that all the evidence presented led to the conviction. It also means that his defending team would have argued their case for a 'not guilty' verdict. At the start of the trial, when the defendant first walked into the court room, he was 'innocent until proven guilty'. In this case, justice was done for the victim's family when the jury, after considering the evidence, made the judgement that the defendant was 'found guilty' of the crime because the evidence was examined. So the Paper headline 'Found Guilty' was the more accurate.

Newspapers and the media play an important role in our society highlighting injustice and wrongdoing. They can be a catalyst for change. For example, *The Guardian* published a number of articles about the Windrush Generation scandal, reporting on unfair deportations. The story took off and brought about change at the highest level. However, sometimes the press hacks seem to be intent on a witch hunt, where assumptions are presented as facts. An example of this is the case of Christopher Jefferies. He was a retired schoolteacher from Bristol, who was arrested on suspicion of the murder of a young woman, Joanne Yeates. The reporting in this instance led to a tabloid press frenzy, where around forty articles were published about him. Many newspapers portrayed him as 'a sexual monster', or a 'perverted voyeur', who used teaching as a means of feeding his perversion. He was portrayed as guilty but later found to be 'not guilty'. It was character assassination based on limited assumptions. He was found to be entirely innocent of any involvement and released without charge.

The real murderer was brought to justice and Jefferies won libel damages from eight newspapers.

So, why am I telling you this? It is a challenge to you not to set yourself up as judge and jury in situations you encounter. At times, when we become dissatisfied with someone, it can be easy to start criticising and complaining to others. It's a cheap option to gossip rather than try and understand. Inaccurate talk can lead to rumours, which influence perceptions and diminish our wider perspective of the person.

Let us not judge people based on secondhand knowledge or gossip because we can never really understand a person unless we are willing to follow their journey, and maybe at times even join them on it.

Rejection

"He came to that which was his own, but his own did not receive him"

(John 1.11 NIV).

You can try to avoid it, but at some stage you will be rejected. Rejection is almost unavoidable because each of us craves closeness and opportunity. Every successful person has experienced rejection. The author J K Rowling was turned down 12 times before she found a publisher for the first *Harry Potter* book. Walter Disney was fired by a newspaper for lack of creativity, even his *Mickey Mouse* cartoons were rejected because they were deemed to be 'too scary for women'. Being turned down is like a punch to the emotions, the pain and disappointment hurt us and can cause us to falter, lose hope and self-confidence.

Entering a romantic relationship there is always a risk of rejection. We are all designed to be connected, secure in love, to be accepted, and treasured for who we are. The road of love is full of potholes and it's path is not always as smooth as hoped. Sometimes, relationships crash before the desired destination is reached.

Rejection is a private anguish that can be just as disabling as physical pain, it can inflict damage to our psychological wellbeing and destabilize our self-esteem. Being rebuffed or spurned will be part of our journey in life. No one escapes the pain of rejection including the Son of God.

Jesus, as a man, was rejected by his own people, scorned by the crowds, mocked and insulted by soldiers, let down by his disciples and at one stage forsaken by God. Jesus understood the despair and internal suffering rejection causes. In Christ, we have a High Priest who has experienced the raw hurt of rejection, and who understands our heartache.

Prayer:
Lord Jesus, I bring to you moments of rejection I have suffered, past and present, the pain that has dented my self-esteem, set me back, and marred my ability to be the person you intended. I pray you fill me with your Spirit, implant in me the knowledge that I am a valued child of God. Come, Lord, pour your Spirit into my heart, touch me, heal and restore me.

Amen.

Re-evaluate

"'Come, follow me,' Jesus said, 'and I will send you out to fish for people.' At once they left their nets and followed him,"

(Mark 1:17-18 NIV).

A friend of mine worked for an international helicopter manufacturer for which he was paid rather well for his time and skills. Every morning, his first responsibility was to switch on this rather complicated machine. This took him all of two minutes, pressing all the right buttons in the correct sequence. After that, for the next one/two hours, he had to stay there monitoring various dials and indicators while this machinery warmed up. While this process took place, he would become very bored. Yes, well paid – but extremely boring. He would sit there wondering, 'Am I wasting my life?' Was this what he really wanted? Was this God's plan for his life? Was what he was doing of real value?

There were elements of his job he found interesting, and it came with a good salary. The money did bring a certain threshold of satisfaction and comfort. However, he remained unsettled and unfulfilled in his position. He wondered if God had something else for him.

It's so easy to settle in one place, feeling secure, comfortable and safe. That's why, at times, we need to be either bored, disturbed or pushed to ask the questions. Does God have something new for me?

Going back to my friend's dilemma at the engineering company. For another couple of years he continued to tussle with the above question. Was he just following the money or was there another calling? After careful thought, prayer and research, he resigned his position as an engineer. Now, a few years later, after re-training, he is a Church of England minister. Materially poorer, but spiritually richer.

In Mark's Gospel Jesus said to the brothers, Simon and Andrew, 'Follow me.' As soon as they left their work and followed him, their lives changed forever.

Revenge

"Do not repay anyone evil for evil. Be careful to do what is right in the eyes of everyone. If it is possible, as far as it depends on you, live at peace with everyone. Do not take revenge, my dear friends, but leave room for God's wrath, for it is written: 'it is mine to avenge; I will repay,' says the Lord. On the contrary: 'if your enemy is hungry, feed him; if he is thirsty, give him something to drink. In doing this, you will heap burning coals on his head. Do not be overcome by evil, but overcome evil with good'."

(Romans 12:17-21 NIV).

Northern Ireland was a troubled place between 1968-1998. There were over 3,500 deaths and more than 30,000 were injured. The Unionists (mainly protestant) wanted to remain within the UK and the Republicans (predominantly Catholic) wanted a united Ireland. It became a sectarian conflict that saw paramilitary organisations rise up. An eye for an eye revenge killing was the norm. Communities lived in fear of the terrorists and families were ripped apart by the deaths of loved ones. The security forces brought in to control the violence patrolled in armour-plated vehicles and were targeted too. No gunman or bomb-maker worked in isolation and the paramilitary had informers and sympathisers willing to contribute to their activity. No man is born a killer, so what motivates a person to become involved in such barbaric acts?

In Colin Breen's book, *A Force Like No Other*, he suggests there is a fanatic ideology at the core of these groups, but as the circle of recruits widens, the central vision weakens, and other motivations come into play including personal revenge. Owen Connolly, a World War II veteran who flew more than thirty bombing missions over Germany with the Royal Air force, brought about the assassination of a prison governor. Owen, an ex-RAF man and retired civil servant, once worked at Stormont, the parliament buildings in Northern Ireland. Connolly informed the IRA terrorist organisation of the governor's address and morning routine and they arranged his assassination. Not only did Connolly become an informer, but he also put the murderers up at his house the day before and hid them after the murder was done. The question is what motivates a man to jeopardise his family's future in such a way? The answer is revenge. Connolly, when he had worked for the civil service, became disgruntled because he believed he should have been promoted to a higher position.

Revenge is a tinderbox. It is an emotional prowling tiger looking for its prey. Unleashed, it can start a chain of events that disrupts, maims, or, at its extreme, kills. Often it is aimed at people, but companies, institutions and governments become victims too. The emotion of revenge can circulate around the body like poison, corrupting and eroding the goodness in us and producing hate. It is fuelled by a personal value system that works according to 'my rules', 'my perception' of how the world should relate to me. I have been 'done in', 'ripped off', 'insulted', 'hurt', 'betrayed, 'undervalued'; the list goes on. Revenge can become an all-consuming force which installs the perceived victim as law maker, judge, jury and enforcer. Maybe this is what happened in Owen Connolly's case?

I would suggest that each of us will feel the anger of revenge bubbling up within us at some time. How we handle this difficult, ever-changing emotion is one of the things that defines us. The Bible gives an instruction of how to cope with it – a hard message. Today's passage is easier to read than live out.

Rock Soul Song

"I know your deeds, your hard work and your perseverance. I know that you cannot tolerate wicked people, that you have tested those who claim to be apostles but are not, and have found them false. You have persevered and have endured hardships for my name, and have not grown weary. Yet I hold this against you: you have forsaken the love you had at first"

(Revelation 2:2-4 NIV).

The concert had awesome special effects, which I think were supposed to be a backdrop to the music. However, the technical brilliance of the stage show overshadowed the band and music. Of course, they played their hit songs, interspersed with new renditions from their latest album. It was a good night. I clapped and sang along with 60,000 others. Of course, the atmosphere was brilliant.

The next day when people asked me about the concert, I would rave about the stunning video and lighting effects but not the music. In fact, I could hardly recall which songs had been played. Yet, years ago, it was the music and the powerful lyrics that drew me to the band.

I wonder if the Christian message has become like that for you? Firstly, you were drawn to the message of Jesus, but over time the very thing that drew you to Christ has become overshadowed by church life and Christian activity. Once you were full of love and admiration for God. Now your diary is full of church meetings and social action.

I want you to think about the key faith route markers which led you to confess Jesus as your Saviour. Was it a sudden revelation of God's forgiveness of our sins? Or maybe a gradual realisation of God's love over years? Now I ask a simple question. Has that initial message/power of God touching your life faded as you have progressed along the Christian journey?

Have you become like the rock band – all effect and less soul of song?

Roman Power in Jesus' Time

During the life of Jesus, the Jews were once again subjects of a foreign power. At this time Jerusalem was under the power of the Roman Empire. Judah was on the edge of the Roman world, a province controlled by Roman officials. This satellite state was allowed to continue its governmental systems and religious practices but under the watchful eye of Roman governors, known as prefects. These prefects were mainly responsible for maintaining security within their province, ensuring there were no uprisings and imposing taxes that fed the central Roman coffers. Each governor had a small number of troops but if unrest started, they could call on garrisons from the neighbouring province of Syria.

Roman influence and decrees affected Jesus' life even before his birth. When Joseph and Mary had to return to their hometown to register under the decree of the Roman Emperor Octavian, the Romans were not persecuting Jews at this time (this was to come later). Jews were allowed a fair degree of autonomy to administer their own affairs and religious practices. Spiritual freedom came at a price. The Sadducees, who controlled the Jewish Legal Council and the temple in Jerusalem, had to work within Rome's restrictions. The Roman prefect would appoint the high priest. While Romans had the military muscle to impose their dominance. Some resented Roman rule. The Zealots were a fundamentalist terrorist group who violently opposed any Roman influence.

Pontius Pilate, the fifth prefect of Judea had a difficult balancing act to maintain between keeping the Sadducees in line and the Zealots suppressed. It was a powder keg of tension waiting to explode. It was on his watch that the High Priest brought their request for Jesus to be crucified for a change under their law. Pilate found himself trapped between two worlds. He found no reason to condemn Jesus under Roman law, yet he was under pressure from Jewish authorities to put him to death. Pilot tried to wriggle out of the situation by giving the people their say. Crucifixion was a Roman form of punishment intended for criminals and those who fought against Roman influence. Jesus was crucified and died under Roman punishment, but was not found guilty under Roman law.

Secret Rendezvous

"And lead us not into temptation, but deliver us from the evil one"

(Matthew 6:13 NIV).

The marriage.
The passing years.
The disconnection.
The internet.
The fantasy.
The desire.
The intention.
The first meeting
The arrangement.
The risk.
The act.
The enjoyment.
The emotional confusion.
The lie.
The secret rendezvous.
The moments of intimacy.
The double life.
The excitement.
The fear of discovery.
The doubt.
The hotels.
The betrayals.
The regrets.
The guilt.
The friendship.
The sex.
The carelessness.
The discovery.
The confession.
The confusion.
The anger.
The blazing rows.
The consequences.
The apology.

The conversations.
The outworking.
The cross.
The forgiveness.
The passing of time.
The restoration.
Leave it behind.

The marriage continues.

Sex Objects

"But I tell you that anyone who looks at a woman lustfully has already committed adultery with her in his heart"

(Matthew 5:28 NIV).

A few months ago, I was given a lift by a gas engineer. The journey was scarier than a rollercoaster ride. Just in a two-mile journey, every woman walking along the pavement would become the focus of his attention. He would take his eyes off the road, staring at them and making some lustful comment. Each woman was a sex object to be lusted over. This habit that had obviously developed at some stage in his life was now most probably playing out during every journey he made.

A Christian businessman told me he had developed a similar habit. He worked from home and to break the monotony of the day, he would view a bit of porn as some entertainment. In his mindset, he had normalised viewing naked women on the Internet as just part of his daily routine. One of the problems in the above cases is that both men developed the habit of dehumanising women to sexual objects for self-gratification.

Today's Bible verse is uncomfortable for men because it challenges how they can be godly and still be a sexual being. A man's sex drive is not a bad thing, its central to a man's makeup and to reproduction. The challenge for men is to keep their sexual urge in check so as not to allow themselves to view a woman as a sex object against those challenging words of Jesus, 'anyone who looks at a woman lustfully has already committed adultery with her in his heart'. The bridge between healthy acknowledgments of womanhood, to lustfully undressing them in your mind is a fine line. The difference between remaining 'godly' as opposed to 'lustful' can simply be in the way a look is delivered as respectful rather than repeatedly in a self-gratuitous manner over and over again.

God isn't asking men (or women) to dismiss their sex drive. He challenges us to control it, develop habits that are good and wholesome. It isn't wrong to appreciate the difference between male and female. It's just sometimes we take too many second looks!

153

Smith Wigglesworth
Poverty to Empowerment

"All of them were filled with the Holy Spirit and began to speak in other tongues as the Spirit enabled them"

(Acts 2:4 NIV)

In Victorian Britain, life was hard for the Wigglesworth family fighting poverty. At the age of seven, an illiterate Smith Wigglesworth worked twelve hour shifts at a wool mill in Bradford. At this time, he found God's love and became a soul winner. The first person he won to Christ was his mother. Later, his spiritual journey was aided when he met a godly man who taught him biblical doctrine. At eighteen years old he found employment as a plumber. Smith was exceptionally tactless, with an abrupt outspoken manner and explosive temper. However, beneath his hard exterior he had a heart for God and for people.

Smith fell in love with a woman from the Salvation Army called Polly. They faced much opposition to their relationship, but love would lead to marriage. Polly was to be the backbone and the making of Wigglesworth, she taught him to read and write. Together they formed a partnership of encouraging each other in Christian ministry and helping each other in practical ways. He would look after the children while she led church meetings. She supported him with doing the business accounts.

His skills as a plumber were so in demand that he started missing church and his faith cooled, leaving Polly to run the church. His spiritual decline caused tension in their marriage. When his anger started to surface. Wigglesworth recalled, 'I used to go white with rage and shake all over with temper.' After two years, he slowly rediscovered his faith. On Saturday evenings, he would knock on people's doors and share the gospel. He aimed to lead someone to Christ every day.

After attending many divine healing meetings, he started his own healing ministry at the Keswick convention. This was largely unplanned; at short notice he was asked to preach, and at the end of the service, people came to the altar to pray for healing. First up was a man on crutches: Nervously, Wigglesworth laid hands on him and to his astonishment, the man dropped his crutches and leapt up and down. Others were also healed. Returning to Bradford, he began to hold healing meetings. In February 1904, God used him in deliverance when he was called upon to visit a man who was haunted day and night by the images of hanging. Believing it was demonic spirits possessing the man, Wigglesworth and church members exorcised the demons, and as a result, the man surrendered his life to Christ.

Wigglesworth was far from the perfect preacher, he struggled with his stuttering every time he entered the pulpit, but he had an insatiable spiritual hunger for things of God. He heard about a new move of the Spirit in Sunderland in which God's power fell upon people who started speaking in tongues. He was fascinated and wanted to discover more, so he planned a trip to Sunderland. Friends warned him against this desire as they saw it as a satanic manifestation, but he would not be swayed from seeking a gift from God.

His initial visit to Sunderland proved discouraging. At one healing meeting he noted people were wearing glasses and wondered why God didn't heal their sight. After days of meetings, he still hadn't received this new phenomenon called the Baptism of the Spirit, and he became discouraged. However, on his way home, he stopped at the minister's house only to find the minister wasn't there. The clergyman's wife prayed for him. As she left the room to answer the doorbell, the Holy Spirit suddenly fell on him and he was empowered to speak in utterances of the Spirit. He had at last received the baptism of the Holy Spirit. He felt a new purification of his soul. This was to prove a new chapter in his ministry. The following Sunday at his own church, the congregation were amazed; instead of his usual, faltering, stumbling preaching he spoke fluently, and with power.

Stealing

"Anyone who has been stealing must steal no longer"

(Ephesians 4: 28 NIV).

We all have a stereotype image of criminal in our mind. But have you ever asked yourself the following? Have I developed the habit of a thief? And I don't mean have you robbed a bank, extorted money by Internet fraud, or partaken of pickpocketing. What I am talking about are the ways we subtly steal indirectly, justifying little actions that wrongly enable us to gain at someone else's expense? Things like the unauthorised use of someone's work, adding a few extra miles to the travel expense claim, or not recording some small amount of extra income received when filing a tax return

All these are small things we find ways of justifying without much thought:

- Copyrights – it's a one-off, I'm sure they won't mind.
- The extra miles on the claim form – my car is expensive to run and the payment per mile is not enough.
- The annual tax return – a little undeclared cash income isn't going to make a difference to the government's revenue.

We act under camouflage of having convinced ourselves that our small action of personal gain isn't stealing. No one gets hurt and it makes little difference to the other party. Our actions are virtually anonymous, so who cares…?

God does. He wants us to live holy lives, set an example to others, and walk in the path of righteousness. To do so, there is a cost, maybe in time, maybe financially. The cost of following Christ is not just in our more prominent actions but in the small ones too.

Stoning in the Old Testament

"If it is true and it has been proved that this detestable thing has been done in Israel, take the man or woman who has done this evil deed to your city gate and stone that person to death"

(Deuteronomy 17:4-5 NIV).

There are some things in the Bible that are difficult to understand. The practice of stoning is one of them. From our 21st century viewpoint, it's hard to recognise a loving God with this form of punishment. In fact, today, we would now instruct lawyers to take God to court for such a barbaric instruction to try and repeal this law.

It is only from a historical vantage point that we gain some insight into the practice. Stoning in the Old Testament was the most common form of capital punishment prescribed by the Mosaic Law. With no police forces patrolling the nation of Israel, it was up to local tribal leaders in each town to administer justice fairly. The punishment of stoning was a deterrent to discourage unrighteous behaviour and to stop disorder running rampant throughout a nation, a means to purge the community from evil. For someone to be stoned the law required two or more witnesses to testify against a person. If the accused was found guilty and sentenced to death, the stoning usually took place outside the city. It was also the witnesses' duty to throw the first stones before others followed.

Gaining an understanding of the historic context of this form of punishment also gives us an insight into some of the New Testament stories. For example, it explains why many people might have thought that Jesus' execution should be by stoning. It also gives us understanding of the motivation of the religious clerics who wanted to stone women to death for adultery.

Below are a few examples of offences that were punished by stoning.

The Bible references are included to show the origination and are all taken from the *New International Version*

Worship of other Gods:

> If your very own brother, or your son or daughter, or the wife you love, or your closest friend secretly entices you, saying, "Let us go and worship other gods".............. [6] You must certainly put them to death. .... [10] Stone them to death, because they tried to turn you away from the Lord your God,

Deuteronomy 13

Disobedience of a Son:

> [20] He is a glutton and a drunkard." [21] Then all the men of his town are to stone him to death.

Deuteronomy 21:18-21

Adultery:

> If a man is found sleeping with another man's wife, both the man who slept with her and the woman must die. You must purge the evil from Israel.

Deuteronomy 22:22

Child Sacrifice:

> 'Any Israelite or any foreigner residing in Israel who sacrifices any of his children to Molek is to be put to death. The members of the community are to stone him.

Leviticus 20: 2-5

Blasphemy:

> [14] "Take the blasphemer outside the camp. All those who heard him are to lay their hands on his head, and the entire assembly is to stone him.

Leviticus 24:14-23

Plus, an unusual one:

> "If a bull gores a man or women to death, the bull is to be stoned to death."

Exodus 21:28

Stuck in the Bubble

"Blessed are those who mourn, for they will be comforted"

(Matthew 5:4 NIV).

When I moved into my first house, I introduced myself to my neighbour, a lady in her early sixties. I noticed she was wearing a wedding ring, so I asked after her husband. This was her cue to unload her story pouring out a torrent of deep emotion about the loss of her beloved husband. As a young man who had never lost anyone close at that time, I found it difficult to truly empathise, but I did my best to nod in the right places and listen well.

Her husband seemed to have passed away suddenly and her pain was tangible, raw and intense. Her life seemed to have stopped in its tracks at the very point of his death. She was totally distressed and lost without him. I imagined the funeral could have been no more than a few weeks ago, but when she said he'd died over nine years ago, I was rather shocked. I know that the pain from a loved one's death never goes away, but I assumed as time passes the pain doesn't feel so raw. This lady however, seemed trapped in a bubble of time, still totally consumed by the intensity of the loss nine years before. The heavy burden of pain she carried had obviously taken its toll. She seemed to be lost, without hope, with no foundation of faith to stand upon.

The great promise of the Christian message is of life after death. At the crucifixion of Jesus, we see his death brings in real hope in the darkest of times. A hope that conquers death and sin, once and for all. It doesn't mean Christians get to leapfrog the grieving process when someone close to us dies. But it does mean we can have peace when we look back, knowing that our loving creator was there with us, is still with us, and will always be with us as we press on towards the prize of eternal life with him. Losing someone is painful, but we can be certain that our sorrow will turn to joy when we are raised to new life with him.

Prayer:
I pray for those who have lost someone close to them, I pray that you will be their comfort in their moments of despair, be their light in the darkness, be their hope in their mourning.

Amen.

Suspended

"You are my refuge and my shield; I have put my hope in your word"

(Psalm 119:114 NIV).

I am suspended about ten metres from the ground on a ski lift that has temporarily broken down. Today, the temperature, at its best, is minus eight. There is a twenty kilometres per hour Siberian wind blowing through the French valley, and this wind chill factor is making it feel much colder. Even wearing winter ski gear, over a sustained period this would give limited protection against the elements.

The good news for me was the place where I hung suspended had tall pine trees protecting me from the strength of the bitter wind. Of course, I could see the physical effects of the wind as the tops of the trees swayed in the wind. Where I was stranded in mid-air, there was a surreal feeling of calmness as the worst of the wind was held at bay. Of course, I could feel the cold, but there was no immediate danger of me freezing to death.

As a Christian, I don't believe that we constantly live in a protective bubble that stops the troubled winds of change from blowing in our direction, but whatever life throws at us, God is not far away. Romans 10:13 (NIV) says: 'Everyone who calls on the name of the Lord will be saved'. He will be our refuge and shield when the storms of trouble blow our way. Sometimes we just need to sit tight and let him be our protector.

Prayer:
Lord, I thank you that in times of trouble, disappointment and life's challenges, you will be my hiding place and my shield. Be my strength in my weakness, my windbreak from the storm, the solid ground when life becomes shifting sands. Be my guide, my friend and my Saviour.

Amen

Tamar Trauma

"... don't force me! Such a thing should not be done in Israel!
Don't do this wicked thing ..."

(2 Samuel 13:12).

The Bible has the shocking habit of showing life as it is and this passage is not an easy read. It talks about the horrendous crime against Tamar and how she was raped. Sexual violence is an age-old crime, usually perpetrated by men against women. What motivates a man to sexually assault a woman? I find it hard to understand. The psychological, emotional and physical effects of this traumatic event can impact the victim's life for years. Flashbacks and crippling haunting emotions can confine them to a shell and they become just a trace of the person they once were or could have been. In Tamar, the distress, humiliation and pain was very obvious as she wept in torment. But sometimes for those who have been violated, the shame, the self-blaming and the pain they feel is locked in and the key thrown away.

Sex (making love) should always be consensual, never forced. It should be about giving and not about taking. But sadly, this is not always the case. In the UK, Rape Crisis England and Wales say that twenty percent of women between sixteen and thirty-seven have experienced a serious sexual assault or been raped. A truly awful statistic.

Christian men need to make a stand on behalf of women. To be an example of righteousness in a world dominated by sexual gratification. To act respectfully, set high standards and honour female friends, girlfriends and wives. We need to be a light in the world of sexual darkness. An example of gentleness, love, self-giving, holiness, trustworthiness, care, and respect. Sex is about loving, not taking. And if we are in a marriage, showing love the right way becomes the fruit of Kindness and care. Gentleness is born out of intimacy when two become one.

(Suggested reading: Full content: 2 Samuel 13: 1-21)

The Assyrian Empire
(900 BC - 600 BC)

Throughout the Old and New Testament the actions and influences of empires upon one another provided a biblical backdrop. In 2 Kings: 17 (NIV), we witness how the story of the Hebrew kingdoms of Israel and Judah was interwoven with the Assyrian empire.

The powerful Assyrian Empire stretched across the ancient mid-west from the Persian Gulf to southeast Turkey, and from Egypt to modern day Iran/Iraq. Its capital was Nineveh, famous in the Bible for the story of a runaway prophet, who took a roundabout boat trip to the capital, via a ferry and a large fish. The empire was commercially successful, its capital was the 'go to' place of the day with a metropolis arts city boasting its own botanical gardens and zoos. There was also an extensive library containing thousands of clay tablets, many recording the administration records of the kings that had reigned.

Assyrians worshipped the pagan god Ashur. Legend has it that he was the god of war, and when Assyrians conquered nations they promoted his supremacy over other gods. All conquered people enslaved in captivity were made to worship Ashur.

The Assyrian military was well organised and known for their violence and murderous savagery. They were the first military to mass produce iron weaponry for their war machine. This trained army went into battle with chariots and battering rams to smash down city gates. Under the cover of fire from their army's slingers, Assyrian assault troops used scaling ladders to overrun their ememies' defences. They were tactically and technologically advanced compared to their enemies. Their army was feared because when they conquered a city, they would deport large sections of the inhabitants and distribute them throughout the territories of Assyria. This was their policy to prevent any future uprisings in the region. To further dismantle a nation's identity, they re-populated their conquered cities with foreigners and Assyrians.

In 722 BC, the Assyrians conquered Israel and took the people into captivity where they were scattered throughout the population of the Assyrians middle eastern empire. This dismantling of the nation of Israel saw the tribes of Israel lost permanently. Now known as 'The ten lost tribes of Israel'.

God used the Assyrian empire to deliver his judgement on his people who had all but forsaken his holy commandments and started to worship false gods and idols. A succession of rogue kings had done evil in the sight of the Lord. Israel had been ripped to pieces, and now only Judah survived as God chose people.

(Suggested Reading: 2 Kings Chapter 17)

The Babylonians Conquer the Assyrians

The Assyrians tried to hang on to their Empire with the help of Egyptians, but the Babylonians and Medes bulldozed the Assyrian army into history. Nineveh, the capital of Assyria was destroyed in 612BC.

The Babylonians were the new boys in town dominating the region. This was basically the modern-day landmass, from Lebanon through Syria, and Iraq to the sea at Kuwait, reaching the borders of Egypt.

The Babylonians were trailblazers and well educated and many of the population both men and women could read and write. It was also the Babylonians who introduced basic medical procedures and started diagnosing illnesses and their symptoms. Their primary god was *Marduk,* who was the god of heaven and earth and humanity.

King Nebuchadnezzar was running the Babylonian power base and Judah was under threat from his conquest. Judah's, King Jehoiakim, negotiated a 'cash for peace' deal with The Babylonians. This was called 'Tribute money' and its payments ensured Judah survived as a nation.

Jehoiakim initially paid the protection money but after three years he got fed up and refused to continue paying. This didn't go down too well at Babylon HQ, so the Babylonian army marched on into Jerusalem to give the people of Judah a good kicking. To make matters worse, Jehoiakim passed away of natural causes, leaving his eighteen-year-old son, Jehoiachin, to face the music, (2 Kings 24: 8-17 NIV). The Babylonians besieged the city to take control of it, and the young ruler had few options or ideas and capitulated. This was a rather bad day for the king and his people. The craftsmen, academics, officials and fighting men were all taken into captivity to Babylon (south of Baghdad, Iraq), along with the temple artefacts. In all, 10,000 people were forced to uproot and live in captivity. Jerusalem's poor were simply discarded and left behind.

The Babylonian empire lasted less than a century, (625-536 BC) which as empires go, was rather short term. The Persian empire and King Cyrus became the new boys in power.

The demise of the Babylonians was good news for the people of Judah. With King Cyrus in power, God used a couple of fellows called Ezra and Nehemiah to talk the King around to letting the people of Judah return home and repair the Holy city of Jerusalem.

(Suggested reading: 2 Kings Chapters 24-25)

The Bad and the Ugly

"Do not let any unwholesome talk come out of your mouths, but only what is helpful for building others up according to their needs, that it may benefit those who listen"

(Ephesians 4:29 NIV).

Rhian Collins and her fiancé David Read had two young children. She was a slim, smiley, photogenic thirty-year-old who had a job as a psychiatric nurse at a hospital in Swansea. Nursing has its pressures; coping with grumpy doctors, demanding patients, and long night shifts, but something bad and ugly was going on in her life as well, and the outcome was to be fatal, scarring those closest to her for life. The first indication that not all was well was when Rhian's behaviour changed. She became obsessed with her appearance, going to the gym up to four times a day and taking weight-loss pills. But what was it that caused her to take the path she did? Had she become mentally ill, unable to cope with the stress?

It all came to a head when David came home with their children. There he discovered her motionless body, hanged. Rhian had taken her own life and become one of the 6,507 suicides registered in the UK that year. What had happened to this vibrant, attractive woman who shared happy family photos on Facebook? What terrible circumstances had caused a family to be ripped apart by these terrible actions?

After a five-month investigation into the circumstances surrounding her death, it was concluded that Rhian's co-workers had bullied her. They had made her life utterly unbearable.

Bullying and harassment at its extreme can cost lives. Others survive the painful hounding on a daily basis. It can happen in the workplace, in a church setting, even at home. It destroys people from the inside out. Having someone on your back constantly criticising and mocking you, or cyberbullying you can make life extremely difficult. Christians aren't immune from bullying or its effects, which include, anxiety, unhappiness, nervousness and the erosion of a person's confidence and self-worth. Having a faith can attract bullying as many churched children have found out during their school years. Continuing harassment is bad and ugly and damages people. A bully's candle doesn't burn any brighter by blowing someone else's out. Bullying needs to be talked about and the perpetrators must be challenged and stopped.

As Christians we need to be salt of the earth (Matthew 5:13-16 NIV). We need to be willing to intervene and stand up for others. We must also double check the banter and actions we are using ourselves to ensure they are uplifting and not destructive. Ask yourself this challenging question:

Are others suffering from the effect of your words and actions?

Prayer:

Show me Lord if my words or deeds are causing others discomfort. Teach me how I can be a conduit of kindness and reflect your love.

I ask for forgiveness when I fail you, when my careless words inflict pain and suffering on others.

Forgive me Lord when my actions cause unnecessary harm and distress.

Help me Jesus to be a person who is encouraging and righteous.

To the glory of God

Amen.

The Bomb Squad Arrive

I decided to sort out my loft containing those things that one day might be useful. In one dim corner, camouflaged by layers of cobwebs, I found some small boxes left behind by a lodger. As I moved these boxes, I noticed resting on an eave a small pineapple-shaped object. To reach it I had to lie belly flat, and I had to stretch awkwardly to grasp it. To my surprise it was rather heavy and it seemed to be made of metal. I pulled the object towards me and to my horror I discovered I was holding a hand grenade with its safety pin precariously attached. I grasped the release lever firmly as I know by holding the leaver in, it shouldn't detonate. However, I couldn't stay there lying prostrate for long as my grip would be hard to maintain. So, I awkwardly reversed out of the cramped space and somehow managed to grasp the loft ladder one handed and fully secure the safety pin.

With the phone in one hand, the grenade in the other, I called the police and explained my predicament. The operator calmly explained that the police would soon arrive, and a bomb disposal unit would be dispatched. I was advised that it may not be in my best interest to continue to hold it. I was instructed to take the grenade into the garden, ensure the safety pin was in, then carefully place the grenade down and cover it up with as many mattresses as I could find. I did as instructed, nervously returning several times to place more bed mattresses on top of it.

The police arrived, closed the road and told me to evacuate my house. An hour later the bomb squad arrived and suited up in their protective clothing. After examining the object, they confirmed that it was a genuine hand grenade. Then, using specialist equipment, they found that the detonator had been removed and it was more likely to be a collector's piece. The bomb squad took the grenade away, the road was reopened. The drama was over.

When they said it was a collector's piece I remembered that a past lodger had collected war memorabilia. I phoned him.

Me: I found a hand grenade in my loft. Does it belong to you?

Frank: How many did I leave?

Me: How many? You mean there could be more?

Frank: Yes.

Me: How many did you have?

Frank: I cannot remember.

Me: What do you mean you cannot remember!

Frank: I bought them a long time ago.

To cut a long story short, no more hand grenades were found.

Across the world, grenades, landmines are used to murder indiscriminately. To God every life is of value. Many of us, without realising, could be linked to companies that bring harm and suffering to others through armament production and their misuse. Many of us may be enrolled in a pension scheme that buys shares in these companies. Have you ever examined how your pension contributions are invested?

Should we as Christians be more ethically selective about how our pension contributions are used? Are there a few 'grenades' hiding amongst the small print of our retirement funds?

The Comedian

"Though one may be overpowered, two can defend themselves. A cord of three strands is not quickly broken"

(Ecclesiastes 4:12 NIV).

I have several friends who are professional comedians and as I've watched their acts live, I have always been struck by their vulnerability. The solitude of the solo artist standing in the spotlight, centre stage, facing the audience. It's a kind of 'Daniel in the lion's den', with risk of being eaten alive by an audience hungry for fun. The comic's only weapon of survival is a series of jokes, one-liners and anecdotes. If his yarns and gags hit the mark, the comic will soon have them where he wants them... almost laughing on auto-pilot. However, paying pundits are an unpredictable beast, unleashed from the rules of politeness, they become a dangerous wild animal with a tendency for spontaneous interjection, without licence. The one-man act is at the mercy of the audience, and from where I am sitting it looks a lonely and vulnerable place. With skill he can navigate the situation and live to give another performance; but on a bad day when the audience seems far more hostile a foe than friend, it becomes a lonely journey home. Only despondent thoughts recycle through his head to keep him company. There are no assuring words of encouragement, just himself and his mind games.

Professional acting, apart from a one-person show, is a different profession. It's a team game, with all contributing to pull the storyline forward. If an actor veers slightly off the script or has a blank moment, there is a good chance that a fellow actor will pick up the storyline and it will continue unabated and unnoticed by the audience. A good acting troupe will carry and cover for each other in those difficult moments.

If you are in any form of ministry, it requires you to step into a place of vulnerability. Whether you are a street pastor, an event organiser or a church leader, to minister to people is to make yourself both available and vulnerable. The greater the responsibility or public profile, the higher the expectation others have of you and the greater the risk of isolation. Unwittingly, it is easier to become the solo artist than the team player. The higher people climb the tree of public ministry, the greater the risk of isolation.

Moses became an overworked one-man act (Exodus 18:13-26 NIV). Thankfully, his straight-talking father-in-law told him to delegate, get his act together, before he burnt himself out. We all need people to support us and cover us, if we metaphorically get the lines wrong.

My question; Have you become the solo artist holding centre stage or are you working together in the troupe? Remember Jesus sent the disciples out to minister in twos (Luke 10:1 NIV). Working in isolation is a dangerous occupation and if it all goes wrong, the 'joke' will be on you.

The Corrie Ten Boom Story
(1892–1983)

May 1940.

The Dutch Prime Minster, through his radio broadcast tried to reassure a nervous nation that although Germany was at war with France and England, Holland's neutrality would be respected. Five hours later, German bombs fell on Dutch soil. Until that moment, two spinsters' Corrie Ten Boom and her sister Betsie, lived a quiet life as daughters of a watchmaker. At first, the Nazi occupation, brought benefits to the Ten Boom family as German soldiers bought watches to send to loved ones, but slowly they started to inflict acts of anti-semitism; bricks were thrown at Jewish shop windows and signs appeared banning Jews from parks, shops, and restaurants. Soon the Jews were forced to wear yellow stars. Then the disappearances, public arrests and deportations began.

In 1942, one evening just before curfew, a knock on the Ten Boom family's back door was to change their destiny. A woman with a suitcase stood there. She had fled her home and desperately needed accommodation, which they then gave her.

Two nights later, another knock on the door alerted them to the arrival of another Jewish couple. More Jews arrived over time, and the home above the watch shop became a haven for those being hunted by the Gestapo. This Christian family became part of the Dutch resistance, accommodating fugitives until safe houses could be found. However, it was not without risk, so the resistance arranged for a secret hiding place to be built in Corrie's bedroom. A new wall was disguised as an old one, with a secret entrance and enough space behind it for six people to stand. There was an alarm system installed and regular drills in case the house was raided. The Ten Boom family were living a double life, continuing their watchmaking and repair business whilst running an underground ring. Every day they feared that their secret activities would be discovered.

February 1945.

Corrie Ten Boom was in bed, ill with the flu, when suddenly she heard the alarm sound and people rushed past her to the hiding place. After this, German soldiers burst in accusing her of hiding Jews. She and Betsie were both beaten, but they gave away no secrets. The family were detained and transferred to Scheveningen Prison. After endless questioning, Corrie Ten Boom was incarcerated with three others in a small cell, six steps long and two steps wide. Boredom become the enemy as time moved from one week to another. Corrie then developed a heavy fever and was transferred to solitary confinement, her only company were ants searching for crumbs.

After three months the interrogation resumed. But instead of the harsh treatment, it turned out to be gentle persuasion by a surprisingly kind Nazi officer. Corrie gave away little detail but was quick to share the hope of the Christian message. Betsie Ten Boom was also in Scheveningen jail, and it was at the reading of their fathers will, that they were briefly reunited

One day the prisoners were ordered to get their things together, and before long they were marched on to trains. There, Corrie managed reunite with her sister Betsie once more. The train lumbered forward, eventually reaching Vaught concentration camp, Holland.

The days in Vaught were a baffling mixture of good and bad. If a single rule had been broken the entire barracks would be punished by having to stand to role call at 4am. Within the prison Corrie worked in the Philips factory for eleven hours a day soldering relay switches for German fighter planes. The factory prisoner-foreman instructed Corrie to solder the components incorrectly to hinder the German war effort.

As the war turned against Germany, the camp was evacuated by train and eighty women were jammed into carriages like animals ready for slaughter.

The stench of urine and excrement on the two-day journey was almost unbearable. They arrived at Ravensbruck concentration camp, a city of barracks looking like a vast scar on the green German landscape. In the centre, a square smokestack emitted a thin grey vapour. After they had been processed, they were ordered to strip and walk naked to the showers while jeering soldiers looked on, but in the midst of this, God provided a way for the sisters to retain their bible. Their overcrowded barracks were flea infested and the harsh routine of the camp life took its toll on Betsie's health, but she continued to urge Corrie to pray for those around her.

Regular medical inspection brought more humiliation as prisoners were forced to queue naked in front of guards. Corrie drew comfort from the fact that Jesus had shared this humiliation: he had hung naked on the cross too, in front of the mocking crowd. Corrie and Betsie started a bible study, which became a source of comfort to many of the prisoners, who were left to do this undisturbed by the guards who didn't want to venture their way because of the fleas in their barracks!

The cold winter of roll calls were an endurance test that many of the 10,000 women would not survive. Betsie's health gradually deteriorated and eventually she was taken to the camp hospital, never to return. Corrie had lost her sister.

An administrative error saw Corrie released a week before hundreds of women of her age were gassed. The long-disjointed train journey to Holland was a blur, but Corrie finally arrived malnourished at a Dutch hospital. After a period of recuperation, she returned home, but the old house seemed empty without Betsie and Father, and she missed the activity of the underground. Corrie began telling her story at churches. At one meeting she met an aristocratic lady who offered her a fifty-two room mansion for ex-prisoners.

At the age of fifty-three, Corrie began a worldwide ministry which took her to more than sixty countries in thirty-two years. God used her to transform many people's lives by introducing them to Jesus. Corrie's family saved hundreds of Jews from the Nazis. She died on her 91st birthday.

She received many tributes, including being knighted by the queen of the Netherlands. In 1971, she wrote a best-selling book of her experiences during World War II, entitled '*The Hiding Place*', which was turned into a film.

The Data Trail

"Jesus sat down opposite the place where the offerings were put and watched the crowd putting their money into the temple treasury. Many rich people threw in large amounts. But a poor widow came and put in two very small copper coins, worth only a few cents. Calling his disciples to him, Jesus said, 'Truly I tell you, this poor widow has put more into the treasury than all the others. They all gave out of their wealth; but she, out of her poverty, put in everything — all she had to live on'"

(Mark 12:41-44 NIV).

Did you realise that you are creating a personal trail of data that says more about you than most people will ever know? This information you are producing reveals your movements, creates an ongoing record of your lifestyle, and even gives an indication of your passions and character. The good news is that this data remains private, under the lock and key of a sophisticated security system, and is accessible to only a few trusted people. For your personal record, each month you can opt to receive a copy of your transactions with the world in a document called a bank statement. If someone analysed the information, would it give a good impression of you?

Your bank statement is a window into your financial health and lifestyle. It could be littered with standing orders, direct debits, annual subscriptions, mobile phone bills, dispersed amongst necessities like food and fuel bills. Your balance could show your daily struggle to put food on the table for the family, the lack of cash to cover the utility bills and fuel for the car, or show your monthly hire purchase agreement for the computer you bought, so your children can have the opportunity to study and have a better future. At the other extreme, it could show your lump sum investments into the stock and bond market.

Whatever station in life we find ourselves at, being a follower of Christ should change our view on money. For those struggling, it should drive us to prayer; to look to our heavenly Father to provide our needs. It may help to dismantle the solid wall of pride and start the conversation of 'I need help'. It teaches us about the principle of giving, even when in a poor financial place. In the Bible, there is a story about a widow that gave all she had and how much God valued this. The Christian principles we learn when in a difficult place become a habit in times of trial.

175

For those following Christ, the principle of giving should hit our bank balance and curtail our spending power. For those who have much, the challenge is not to focus on maintaining a comfortable lifestyle or to secure a good pension, but to maintain the principle of giving that was taught in the early days. If you want to assess your walk with Christ, just look at the data on your bank statement. It will say more about the price you are willing to pay to follow Christ than anything else. The last part of a man to be converted to the ways of Christ is his wallet.

The Dead Sea Scrolls

You may have heard of *The Dead Sea Scrolls* and wondered what the story is behind them and the significance to our faith.

In 1946, near Qumran in the Judean wildness on the north-western corner of the Dead Sea, a priceless discovery was made by three Bedouin shepherds. While attending their flock one of the young shepherds went to explore the nearby caves in the hope of finding a cache of gold. He discovered two small holes in the rocky craggs, one barely large enough for a cat to enter. He threw a rock into the cavity and heard something break. Later he returned. Crawling inside the cave he found what appeared to be ancient scrolls housed in clay jars. Returning with the other shepherds they unearthed one of the greatest archaeological biblical discoveries of all time. These scrolls would become known as the *Dead Sea Scrolls*, simply because they were found near the Dead Sea. These parchments had been preserved for two thousand years and contained the Hebrew canon of scripture and Jewish historical records.

The significance of finding scrolls was not obvious to the Bedouins at the time, who took them to their encampment where, uncertain of their worth, the manuscripts were stored in a bag and left hanging on a tent pole for several weeks. Occasionally the find was shown to other Tribal people. Eventually, the Bedouin took them to a dealer of antiquities who tried to establish their value. But after several weeks the Bedouin were told they were of no archaeological value and maybe even stolen from a Jewish synagogue. The Bedouin took the scrolls to a market in Bethlehem where they were able to sell the first few to a dealer for few Jordanian pounds. Other scrolls were sold via a third party.

Eventually, it was established by experts that the parchments dated back two thousand years. This prompted a 'scroll rush'. Between 1947–1956 archaeologists and Bedouins searched and successfully found additional scrolls and fragments in eleven separate locations. In all, these scrolls yielded numerous portions from every book of the Old Testament, except Esther. There were Thirty-three scrolls of Deuteronomy and thirty-nine of the Psalms. The Isaiah Scroll was dated one thousand years older than any previously known text. In one cave there were thousands of fragments. The process of piecing them together was a giant jigsaw puzzle. To the horror of modern-day archaeologists, the fragments were stuck together with glue and newly invented Sellotape.

The magnitude of the discovery was overshadowed by the violence in Palestine leading up to the formalisation of the State of Israel in 1948.

Eventually, a comparison between the then known oldest Hebrew manuscripts and the recently discovered Dead Sea Scrolls was made. They found astonishing accuracy of transmission over a thousand-year period. To us, as believers, the Dead Sea Scrolls provide enormous encouragement as they show that God's Scripture has not been watered down over time.

The Death Valley Endurance Test

"Do you not know that in a race all the runners run, but only one gets the prize? Run in such a way as to get the prize"

(1 Corinthians 9:24 NIV).

I once lived in a small town in America's Wild West. Lone Pine, California, is well known for two things – being the gateway to Mount Whitney, the highest mountain in the Lower forty-eight states: and being the gateway to Death Valley, one of the hottest and most hostile places on earth. It is also the lowest point in the Western Hemisphere.

Every July, insane runners from around the world come together for the *Badwater 135*, a 135 mile ultra-marathon that begins in fifty degree Celsius temperatures in Death Valley, 282 feet below sea level. It finishes at an elevation of more than 8,300 feet, halfway up Mount Whitney.

Some runners take it so seriously they have their toenails surgically removed to prevent problems. Others train for the event with a clothes dryer vent blowing a full blast of hot air directly onto their face. I have watched runners being violently sick at the side of the road; many collapse from heat exhaustion and fail to finish. Some can't make it thirteen miles, let alone 135!

What has always intrigued me about this race is how some made it to the finish line and some didn't. I watched a US Marine Corps sergeant, supported by a team of helpers, drop out after a few miles, while a sixty-year-old granddad from England completed the entire race, his wife coaxing him on with a can of his favourite beer dangling from the roof of their car.

I learned an important lesson: the race is not about your age, your occupation, or your physical appearance. It's *all* about endurance. Only those who endure to the very end will break the finishing tape and claim the prize.

Press on! The prize is ahead of you. It is not an earthly prize but an everlasting crown given to those that believe in true endurance. When the going gets tough ... remember, when we finish the race it will take us across a finish line where on the other side we will come face to face with Christ.

Julian Lukins

The Good Book

The Bible will keep you from sin,

or sin will keep you from the Bible."

Dwight L. Moody

(Suggested Bible reading form The New International Version):

2 Timothy 3.16-17.   Hebrews 4.12.   Ephesians 6: 10-18.

The Hebridean Revival
(1942 – 1952)

"To humans belong the plans of the heart, but from the Lord comes the proper answer of the tongue"

(Proverbs 16:1 NIV).

Peggy and Christine Smith were two sisters, who shared a small cottage on the Isle of Lewis. One of the sisters was blind, the other bent over with arthritis. Both grieved for their own parish because no young people attended. They decided that twice a week they would get on their knees and pray for God's Spirit to move in their parish. A Bible verse came to them, 'For I will pour water on the thirsty land, and streams on the dry ground; I will pour out my Spirit on your offspring, and my blessing on your descendants' (Isaiah 44:3 NIV). Some time later, Peggy had a vision and saw the church crowded with young people, and an unfamiliar minister standing in the pulpit. They shared their vision with others and a letter was sent inviting the evangelist Duncan Campbell to come and minister. Initially, he turned down their request, but later changed his mind due to the prompting of the Holy Spirit. He agreed to stay for two weeks. The sisters continued to pray for a revival to fall upon their community.

Mr Campbell arrived one night by mail steamer. Upon landing at the dockside, he was asked if he could speak at a short meeting at the parish church while on his way to his accommodation. Even though he was tired from the long journey, he spoke and such was the move of the Spirit that night that Mr Campbell never made it to his supper! Many meetings followed and people came to faith even before they arrived at the church.

Revival swept through the island like the early days of the Apostles. People were touched by the power of God. On one occasion, over a hundred young people, who were dancing at the local hall, suddenly stopped when the Spirit moved amongst them. The music ceased and within minutes the young people made their way to the church. Other men and women who had gone to bed, got up and headed for the church too. The meeting then continued until 4.00 am. Five of the young men who found Christ that night became ministers in the Church of Scotland.

On another occasion, people started gathering around the police station near to where the prayerful sisters lived. When Mr Campbell was asked to go and preach there he asked, 'The police station? What's wrong?'

'There's nothing wrong. But about 400 people are gathered there, on their knees, crying out to God,' was the reply.

One evening, in a vision, a girl saw a woman in spiritual agony twenty miles away. When Duncan heard this, he jumped onto a motorcycle and found her exactly as he had been told. The words he spoke brought deliverance and introduced the troubled lady to the Saviour.

This revival, which transformed so many lives happened because God answered the prayers of two old and infirm ladies, willing to get on their knees to seek God. When God chose to answer, no human effort could stop it. Mr Campbell's planned stay of two weeks turned into two years.

Are we desperate for God to move in our churches and revive our communities? Or have we got lost in our own plans? Let's pray for revival – of our own hearts, and of our churches and communities.

(Recommend reading: Channel of Revival: A Biography of Duncan Campbell by Andrew A. Woolsey).

The Hungry Wolf

"How good and pleasant it is when God's people live together in unity!"

(Psalm 133:1 NIV)

A group of primary school children were asked to solve a conflict situation between two people that had contrasting needs and were sharing the same space. The scenario was taken from a story that they were very familiar with: Little Red Riding Hood and the wolf.

The first part of their task was to identify the needs of each character in the story. Then, identify why they were in conflict. Finally, they had to propose a solution that created a harmonious and workable environment which they could both peacefully share. Basically, create a win-win solution of shared goals.

The eager young minds set to work on the challenge. It was easy to identify the wolf's need; he was hungry and needed a good meal to survive. The wolf saw Little Red Riding Hood as 'dinner on his plate'. Her need was one of survival too – just staying alive was her goal. The conflict was like a game of chess with one trying to outsmart the other. So how did the children solve the problem?

The children felt that Little Red Riding Hood should not be eaten under any circumstances and the wolf needed a good meal. So, to resolve the differences, they decided to rewrite the fairy tale. It was decided that the wolf would become a vegetarian and Little Red Riding Hood would have an allotment, where she would grow an abundance of vegetables to share with the wolf, so the wolf always had his fill. The primary school children had created a win-win situation, where conflict was replaced by harmony in a shared space.

Matthew 5:9 (NIV), says 'Blessed are the peacemakers, for they will be called children of God'.

How do we create harmony when there is conflict?

The Idiot

"By the seventh day God had finished the work he had been doing; so on the seventh day he rested from all his work. Then God blessed the seventh day and made it holy, because on it he rested from all the work of creating that he had done"

(Genesis 2:2-3 NIV).

I have to be honest with you, there are certain people I find rather annoying, particularly those undiagnosed workaholics. They have character traits that I find really irritating, especially when they start telling me how many hours they have to work to keep the company or the organisation going. Their phraseology can include, 'If I don't do it, no one will', so their only solution is to work even harder. Adopting the position of linchpin yet with a tendency to moan about the situation. I have even met the occasional workaholic who has not had a holiday for years. And when I enquire why, the reply is 'I'm just too busy' or 'There is so much to do'. When I encounter these kinds of folk, I feel a compelling urge to call them 'an idiot' and tell them to stop being a self-made hero.

In Genesis, we read about God forming the world and humanity. Yet on the seventh day he stopped and rested and reviewed his work. I believe rest is one of the foundation principles set out by God. A time of reflection, time to just stop, a time to not be known for what you do. A time to just, Be!

Of course, there are times when we need put in a good shift or two when a deadline is looming, but temporary pressures should not become patterns without rest. I wonder if a workaholic's motivation is generated from a position of poor self-esteem and inner need? Deep down they are saying, 'Look at me, look at my success, look at what I have achieved.'

On the contrary, a true servant-hearted person will just get on with the job, and knows when to rest and reflect. They work hard and rest well. Mr Workaholic doesn't know or understand the principle of resting. He is blind to the damage his endless businesses create. He could be standing as an obstacle for the employment of others, robbing his family of quality time.

The reason I think a workaholic is an idiot is because they miss the 'full stops' and continue the sentence unpunctuated. Is it time you put a few punctuation marks into your lives? Moments of reflection, time relaxing, and knowing your value with God.

The King of the Castle

"A dispute also arose among them as to which of them was considered to be greatest. Jesus said to them, 'The kings of the Gentiles lord it over them; and those who exercise authority over them call themselves Benefactors. But you are not to be like that. Instead, the greatest among you should be like the youngest, and the one who rules like the one who serves. For who is greater, the one who is at the table or the one who serves? Is it not the one who is at the table? But I am among you as one who serves.'"

(Luke 22:24-27 NIV).

We have all met them, the people who get a little power and it all goes to their heads. They are on company boards, members of our committees, in our workplaces. In fact, they have this annoying habit of springing up in all walks of life including church leadership. Wherever there is a position of power, there is the opportunity for over dominance and abuse of position.

These people, left unchallenged, can start to become the king of their own citadel. Their throne of Lordship enables them to dictate and control situations from their lofty position. These 'Kings of their Castles' might feel strong but could be oblivious to the fact that their associates/friends have become weary of their ways and are withdrawing to their own outposts. The misuse of power has so alienated them that they have little motivation to engage either as a friend or colleague. *Mr Power* has become the King of the Castle, who no one is either listening to or wants to follow.

The values of the Kingdom of God are not about lording over people but are of servanthood and relationship, cheering people on rather than criticising them, laying down our lives and ideas at the cross for the unity of the body of Christ. It is a godly person who can remain humble and responsible with power.

Prayer
Lord, I come to you and ask whatever power or influence I have over others, that you will teach me to use it well, not to mishandle it, or cause unnecessary discouragement and hurt. I pray that I will know that you are the 'King' and I am just a servant in the body of Christ. Help me to follow you and serve well.
Amen.

The Ministry of the Mundane

"You, my brothers and sisters, were called to be free. But do not use your freedom to indulge the flesh; rather, serve one another humbly in love"

(Galatians 5:13 NIV).

Sometimes the way 'ministry' is portrayed from the pulpit seems disconnected and unachievable for the average church punter. Sometimes Christian conference speakers giving entrepreneurial style success stories of ministry achievement can leave us either inspired, or feeling inadequate and even a failure of faith.

I ask a question: Amongst all the hype, have we lost the basic message of servanthood?

In the book of Mark 9: 33-37 (NIV), it describes how an argument broke out amongst Jesus' disciples about who was the greatest. Jesus called the twelve and said, 'Anyone who wants to be first must be the very last, and the servant of all.'

In life, accomplishing menial tasks does not often set the imagination on fire, but they are the bread and butter of life in a Christian community. At our church, each Sunday morning various teams of people arrive early, some put out chairs, others complete sound checks, then there are folk who arrange the tea and coffee. Children's workers prepare for the young people. The AV man rehearses the PowerPoint presentation. It's a hive of activity that the majority of church members rarely see. It's a labour of love *done by a few for the majority.* Without their backstage efforts there would be no projected songs, no PA for the speaker or a balanced sound mix for the worship, no children's activities or refreshments. In fact, the whole operation would be a total shambles.

Servant-hearted people like this are rarely mentioned, yet they are the very glue that bonds the community together. I would suggest they are the real heroes of the faith. These people who are willing to take on the small tasks on a regular basis may seem like the 'Ministry of the Mundane', but it is the outworking of their devotion to Christ that allows others to have a good experience of worship.

Who is the greatest, the one who eats at the table or the one who serves at it?

The Nagasaki Christians

The Japanese city of Nagasaki is well known because it had an atomic bomb dropped on it that helped to end the Second World War. However, this was not the first time some of their people had suffered. Christians back in the seventeenth century suffered torture and an estimated two thousand were martyred for their faith.

Christianity first came to Japan in 1549 when Jesuit missionaries arrived from Portugal and set about converting the locals. Nagasaki became a Christian city with its own parishes and at its peak there were about 500,000 people who identified themselves with the Christian faith. As the message fanned out and more found Christ, the central government saw the rapid rise as a threat and decided to crack down on Christianity.

At the beginning of this campaign, twenty-six foreign missionaries were crucified. In 1614 a national ban on Christianity was enforced and foreigners were expelled from the country. The remaining believers were left to face real persecution. The government came up with a system to publicly root out the embedded Christian faith.

The solution was called 'The Fumie'. It was a wooden board inlayed with brass or stone with the image of Jesus crucified and was taken around the city. It was mandatory that every person had to trample on the figure. For a believer, the image of Christ was divine; to do this was totally abhorrent. To step on the Fumie was to deny Christ. Many Christians did step on the Fumie but continued to practise their faith in secret. However, those who refused were tortured. The aim was not to kill the Christians but to re-educate them. Sometimes the brutality was so severe that it brought the persecuted very near to the point of death. At this stage they were then nursed back to health by doctors, only for the physical infliction to start again with aim of getting them to renounce their faith. Methods of torture included hanging them upside down over a pit filled with excrement. To ensure they would not die from blood to the head they cut slits around their temples to release the pressure. Many practising Christians still refused to denounce their faith, and some were killed by being put in boiling hot springs.

This 'Fumie' became an annual event to root out Christians, With the foreign missionaries banished or murdered the local believers had no outside contact with other Christians for 200 years. The faith was simply passed from one generation to another. It was not until the late nineteenth century that the introspective Japanese re-engaged with the world and religious freedom was restored. Catholic believers came out of hiding and were allowed to build their own Cathedral. It was a miracle that their faith had survived such long-lasting and persistent persecution.

Today, only one per cent of the population are Christians and the community of believers in Nagasaki is the biggest in the country. Ironically, Christianity survived in Japan because of those who decided it was better to be a secret believer than a dead martyr who refused to publicly denounce their faith.

The Name is on the Van

"You yourselves are our letter, written on our hearts, known and read by everyone,"

(2 Corinthians 3:2-3 NIV).

When I ran my own small company, I had my van sign written advertising the name of my business and trade. There it was for all to See; 'Barry Boyton Electrical Services.' Wherever my van went, so did the mobile advert and it was to me surprisingly successful at spreading the word of the services I offered. In fact, I picked up a number of jobs from clients who saw my van parked in supermarket car parks.

Having my name so publicly displayed changed my driving behaviour, especially when it came to interaction with other drivers. If another driver pulled out in front of me or did some risky manoeuvre, I wanted to show my anger at their stupid driving by blasting my horn. However, because my name was plastered all over my van, I couldn't just emerge as an unidentifiable road user letting off steam, as they would know who I was.

The name on the van brought me accountability and I become more self-restrained. At junctions I became more gracious, offering other motorist right of way regularly. In fact, I doubt if other motorist really noticed my change because I just blended into the flow of traffic.

Being a Christian is representing Jesus, and the way we conduct ourselves is noticed by others. If we are fair, and show patience and kindness, people will notice. If we are full of anger, we swear and are unforgiving, people take note. You are a walking advert for Christ and his church. Sometimes it's not what you do but what you don't do that counts. Every interaction with people is a witness to the Gospel. You have his name written on your heart you are God's showcase advertisement to a hurting world. You may be the only 'bible' people will ever read!

Prayer:
Lord help me to be a witness to you in my actions and words. Let the light of your life shine through me to others.

Amen.

The Nicest Person in the World

"But solid food is for the mature, who by constant use have trained themselves to distinguish good from evil"

(Hebrews 5:14 NIV).

My new neighbour became totally distraught and found himself struggling with suicidal thoughts when he discovered his bank account had been hacked and thousands of pounds stolen. He had recently sold his house and was renting as a stop gap whilst he looked for a suitable property for his disabled wife. To add to this distress, the person who defrauded him was someone he trusted – his daughter's partner. My neighbour told me, "He was one of the 'nicest people' you could ever meet." However, beneath the charismatic veneer was a man who had a secret drug dependence and needed cash to feed his habit. Unbeknown to my neighbour, while he had been visiting him, he had been slowly gathering details of his bank account and after finding the passwords, managed to gain access to it. Suddenly, he disappeared, leaving my neighbour, his daughter and her child in limbo. The police investigated and confirmed the culprit but by then it was too late, he, and all the money were long gone. My neighbour's world had been ripped apart, on the verge of retirement he knew he would never recover financially. All this damage was done by one person who seemed to be 'one of the nicest people in the world'.

There are a lot of people who are hiding behind a mask of courteous pleasantries, disguising their secret addictions and harmful acts: the alcoholic, drinking away the family savings, the paedophile causing irreparable harm, or the employee funding a habit by pilfering some of the money they are accountable for.

We need to pray regularly for the gift of discernment, to train our minds and listen to the Spirit of God so we can distinguish good from evil.

Prayer:
Give me wisdom and the ability to listen to your voice of discernment, that I may clearly hear alarm bells when all is not right. Help me distinguish between whom to trust and whom to guard against. Help me, Lord, not to become a victim of broken trust.
Amen.

The Path of Lament

Have you ever felt entirely and utterly alone? Abandoned, broken, bruised? Have you ever felt desperate, as you watch your world fall apart? Have you ever cried a river of tears fearing that you won't be able to stop? Well, you are not alone. The first sound any of us ever made was a cry.

Brokenness is part of our world. To cry is human, tears and sorrow are part of all of our lives. The Bible gives us a way to pray that helps us navigate our pain and brings us closer to God. It shows us how to lament. Lament is the cry of our heart expressed to God. It is more than just the expression of sorrow or the venting of emotion. Through lament, we talk to God about our pain. The Bible is full of lament, but we tend to gloss over it, looking for the positive parts that make us feel better. But if we learn to lament, to let out our pain within the safety of God's loving arms, it will make us feel better and deepen our relationship with God, pull us closer into his heart! Prayers of lament offer us relief. They give us hope in the darkest of times.

As Jesus hung on a cross, pouring out his pain, he quotes Psalm 22 (NIV), as he is about to die. He says, 'My God, my God, why have you forsaken me?' Psalm 22 is one of the greatest examples of a prayer of lament, and Jesus chose it for some of his last words.

We have a God who knows what it is like to suffer. Jesus lived and died as a man. He knew sadness, grief, sorrow, loss. He saw his friends turn away from him, and on the cross in that moment, he could have stayed silent, but he showed us a better way. He showed us the way of lament, for as we lament, we are no longer hiding or pretending. We are real and raw, and in that moment, God can reach us in the middle of our distress.

Society often says 'pull ourselves together'. We pray only happy and hopeful prayers, because we think that's what God wants from us ... but that is a mistake. God wants the real you, not the mask you wear. The path of lament shows us that instead of backing away from God during a hard time or a dark night, we face the pain and worship him with it. As an act of love, we offer it all to God. We lay everything before him.

Sarah Horder

192

The Point of Admission

I acknowledged my sin to you and did not cover up my iniquity. I said,
"I will confess my transgressions to the Lord."
And you forgave the guilt of my sin.

(Psalm 32:5 NIV).

I wonder how many judges, barrister and solicitors would be out of work if people who had knowingly done wrong admitted it? I am sure that hours of court proceedings would be saved if a confession were forthcoming without the pressure of intensive questioning or a trial.

Coming to the point of admission, owning the problem, is a difficult one. It hits against our pride – our natural reaction to self-justify or deny. To be seen in a bad light is not a comfortable experience and, in some cases, to admit failure can have serious repercussions personally: the extremes being loss of a job, a broken relationship or even imprisonment. Fortunately for most of us, our misdemeanour will not lead to time spent under lock and key.

I once saw a play called *People Places and Things*, it was about a young woman who had self-admitted to a drug rehabilitation centre. The play revolves around the main character's self-denial that she was addicted to drugs and the caring staff trying to bring her to the point where she could accept it. The main character blamed other factors – her up-bringing and the pressure of work. It is a story of someone who is fighting hard not to see the true reflection of herself in the mirror. It is a painful play to watch and I felt frustration with her blindness to her problems yet empathised with her struggles. As the play runs through the chaos of her life she slowly starts to see the true reflection, the uncomfortable truths, the wrong she has done, the people she has hurt. Eventually, she reaches the point where she finally admits she has a drug addiction.

Like the woman in the play, you may try to self-justify your wrong actions. You might hide sin behind a façade of smiles and actions, or live life in a cloud of self-denial. But to truly walk with God, we must be a community of people who are open to our sin in its entirety. Christ calls us to confess our sin (1 John 1:9 NIV). We must reach the point of both admission and confession so that forgiveness can begin.

193

The Potential Explosion

"Make every effort to live in peace with everyone and to be holy ... and that no bitter root grows up to cause trouble and defile many"

(Hebrews 12:14 NIV)

There's a saying, 'This job would be great if it wasn't for the people'. Whatever you're doing today there is the possibility of coming into conflict with someone. It may be a very minor disagreement or lead to a blazing row. A confrontation with your teenaged son or daughter, or disagreement with a work colleague or your employer, can easily develop to a level higher than intended.

Conflict is not wrong. It can be a positive thing to embrace, as it challenges us and can help us develop christian characteristics, such as love, patience and peacemaking. It helps us exchange ideas and explore faith, but so often minor disagreements grow into wars, where points of view and positions become entrenched. All unresolved disputes are likely to fester with the passing of time and relationships will suffer.

Disputes among believers are not uncommon. The early church had its fair share of trouble. The Apostle Paul wrote despairingly to the church, calling for them to get their act together:

'I say this to shame you. Is it possible that there is nobody among you wise enough to judge a dispute between believers?' (1 Corinthians 6:5 NIV).

I would like to suggest that most conflict has its roots in unmet needs. A personal agenda that is not being fulfilled.

When you have conflict, you have anger,

When you have anger, you have blame.

When you have blame, you have resentment.

When you have resentment, you have trouble.

When you have trouble, you have conflict.

Conflict is a circle, that if left unbroken becomes a self-generating force that increases in intensity until one day, it explodes, either internally or outwardly causing huge damage to you or someone else.

Dealing with a disagreement is important for our wellbeing. Deep relationships are often formed out of resolved conflicts. Relationships are strengthened where biblical principles are applied for the common good and compromises are made. Below are some biblical principles to aid us in achieving this next time we find ourselves in a situation where conflict might be brewing.

"A gentle answer turns away wrath, but a harsh word stirs up anger"
(Proverbs 15:1 NIV).

"Gracious words are a honeycomb, sweet to the soul and healing to the bones"
(Proverbs 16:24 NIV).

"Do nothing out of selfish ambition or vain conceit. Rather, in humility value others above yourselves"
(Philippians 2:3 NIV).

The Raid

"But Jesus went to the Mount of Olives. At dawn he appeared again in the temple courts, where all the people gathered around him, and he sat down to teach them. The teachers of the law and the Pharisees brought in a woman caught in adultery. They made her stand before the group and said to Jesus, 'Teacher, this woman was caught in the act of adultery. In the Law Moses commanded us to stone such women. Now what do you say?' They were using this question as a trap, in order to have a basis for accusing him. But Jesus bent down and started to write on the ground with his finger. When they kept on questioning him, he straightened up and said to them, 'Let any one of you who is without sin be the first to throw a stone at her.' Again he stooped down and wrote on the ground.

At this, those who heard began to go away one at a time, the older ones first, until only Jesus was left, with the woman still standing there. Jesus straightened up and asked her, 'Woman, where are they? Has no one condemned you?' "No one, sir,' she said. 'Then neither do I condemn you,' Jesus declared

'Go now and leave your life of sin'"

(John 8:1-11 NIV).

The Pharisees mainly lived a life separated from their society; they were a religious party who zealously studied the teachings of Moses and followed their own traditions. Threatened by Jesus and his teachings, they tried to entrap him. Their question was about the woman caught in an act of adultery. What seems odd to me is that she is 'caught' in the very act of adultery. It sounds like a bit of a set-up, maybe someone was spying on her, monitoring her movements and reporting back.

You can imagine the scene that morning: suddenly, the house is raided by a mob, the door is kicked in and they rush into the bedroom to find her naked in bed with someone who is not her husband. She is dragged from the building. She is in a state of shock and very vulnerable, she is marched into another building, she is thrown down, exposed and weeping, at the feet of the waiting male Pharisees. They condemn her to a death by stoning for her sin. This was in accordance to the Law of Moses. But then one of Pharisees spots an opportunity, a means of discrediting their adversary, Jesus; the man who is undermining their teachings by opposing their interpretation of the law. They forcefully drag the woman to Jesus, with the intention of trapping him with a complicated dilemma, which would surely discredit him in front of the crowds. 'In the law of Moses, it commands us to stone such a woman. Now, what do you say?' They are certain they have him on the ropes. If Jesus says, 'the woman should *not* be stoned', they can accuse him of violating the law of Moses. If he calls for her execution, they can report him to the Romans, because Jews did not have the right to carry out their own executions. They are certain of a knockout punch ... but Jesus pauses for a moment, then strikes back with a counterargument that challenges their own façade – *their* sin and self-righteousness. Jesus replies, 'If anyone of you is without sin, let him be the first to throw a stone at her.' It is a moment in which the Pharisees know that they are truly beaten.

Rather than any further condemnation of the traumatised woman, she receives words from Jesus offering her a new start and instructions to take a 180° turn and leave her life of sin. She must now choose which way to go.

The story is a powerful one, a double-edged sword. One blade slicing through our collective self-righteousness and exposing that we are all flawed. The other cutting to the point where each of us is challenged to change our sinful ways.

Prayer:
I admit that I am a flawed person and for all my strengths, all my abilities, all the good things I do, there are still faults. I pray that your Holy Spirit will show me how to make that 180° turn and embrace the way of discipleship.

Amen.

The Red Button

Do you ever worry that one day, despite all your strengths, you will only be known for your big mistakes and failings? Every so often that fear plays out in my dreams. The reason for my fear is that I am aware that embedded deep within my being are several self-destruct buttons. These big red buttons are clearly marked, *'Do not press'*. If one is hit, it could cause a calamitous explosion that will destroy everything I've achieved and all the contentment I have found. An apocalypse caused by my own foolishness, a moment of ill judgement or an irrational reaction. My fear is that a wrong action won't just blow the windows out, it will bring the building crashing down. The consequences will send sharp shards of debris flying and injuring others. A chain of events, that damages my family, leaves my name in tatters, harms the ministry, and brings disgrace to the name of Jesus.

I believe each one of us has these *'Do not press'* buttons. Some, if activated, have limited consequences and the outcome is more a feeling of personal disappointment. However, other larger buttons are far reaching and are driven by undercurrents including money, sex and power. Sadly, I have met many people who have made serious mistakes, some of them are in prison for hitting that red button. Joseph was one of them; he allowed his red button to be pushed on a drunken night out. He got a life sentence for killing someone in a fight with a single punch.

Each of us has the ability to blow it – lose the plot and explode. It may not be in the public domain and the consequences may not linger, but we all have those buttons, and there are plenty of triggers for them. It is only by the grace of God that we survive. John Bradford, the English protestant clergyman and reformer (1510-1555), said after seeing a group of prisoners being led to execution, 'There but for the grace of God, go I.'

Prayer:
Lord I am aware of my weakness, my own ability to get things wrong in both words and actions. I pray that in times of temptation and pressure you will prevent me from pressing the self-destruct button. I acknowledge it is only by the grace of God that I stand. Help me to know your way, and give me wisdom, patience and endurance in all that I do and say.

Amen.

The River

"God is our refuge and strength, an ever-present help in trouble. Therefore we will not fear, though the earth give way and the mountains fall into the heart of the sea, though its waters roar and foam and the mountains quake with their surging"

(Psalm 46:1-3 NIV).

Some years ago, myself and a group of friends went canoeing down a gorge in France. The stunning scenery made for an idyllic afternoon, and we lazily paddled downstream with the gentle current. But it wasn't long before the gorge became narrow, and the water's pace increased. Rocks appeared, at first small ones, and then bigger as the river surged its way down into the gorge. At first, I managed to navigate a way through, but the river got the better of me and I soon lost all control. Sprayed by the powerful waters, I couldn't even see what was coming up next and I became sandwiched between two boulders. Heart racing and battered by the swirling waves, I was going nowhere fast. Thankfully, an instructor managed to pull me free, but I was soon turned 180° by the water and proceeded to float backwards down the river. Utterly exhausted by this point, the current grew calm again and I managed to turn my boat around. The finish line was in sight! My friends were getting out of their boats and were ecstatically shouting, 'that was fun!'. I wondered if I had been on the same trip. I was a broken man.

Is your life journey like my canoeing experience? There are times of peace and happiness. But there are also times of turbulence, fear, and feeling completely out of our depth, with no control over what's happening to us. But as Christians, we can know for certain God's words to us in Psalm 46 NIV, are true; we might feel out of control, but God is our ever-present help in times of trouble. We might feel scared, but we have nothing to fear when we know our loving Father never leaves us for a second. Our life might truly feel like it's falling apart, but we have a God who keeps his promises, and we can trust him to be there, knowing that he's saved us from the biggest problem we'll ever face, our own sin. I needed an instructor to rescue me from the waters that day. But Jesus has already rescued us by his blood on the cross. Whatever we face, in Christ we have nothing to fear.

The Speed Boat Plan

"Do not wear yourself out getting rich; do not trust in your own cleverness"

(Proverbs 23:4-5 NIV).

We sat drinking coffee and he told me his story. I had to admire his audacity and plan of how to 'Get Rich Quick.' He was an entrepreneur in the extreme, equipped with the determination to pull off the 'Big Deal.' He knew his market, he had made contact with the supplier, he had established his clientele and method of distribution. He had done profit and loss calculations on the back of a cigarette packet and it all pointed to a sure winner. Surely nothing could go wrong?

There were logistics problems to overcome, that went with any international import business. The twenty-one mile stretch of water that separated England from France was no obstacle in his mind, nothing that a speedboat couldn't overcome. There were risks of course, but as long as he could stay under the radar of 'HM Revenue and Customs' and the UK police, he had a lucrative enterprise. So, under the cover of darkness, from near the White Cliffs of Dover, England. He set off for France, or to be more precise, he pointed his speed boat in the general direction of France and headed full throttle in a straight line across the busiest shipping channel in the world. He was so confident of his plan that he didn't bother with any satellite navigation. Amazingly, on his first two trips he found the coastline of France and successfully rendezvoused with his supplier. On returning to home soil, he successfully sold his merchandise for a profit of about £100k. So far, so good. his business venture was a roaring success.

Everything changed when he landed his third consignment of drugs. Suddenly, a police helicopter swooped low, lighting up the scene, and armed police came out of the shadows. It was game over. He complained to me, as we sat talking in the prison chapel, that someone had tipped the police off.

Money and greed are talked about throughout the entire Bible. In fact, Jesus talked about this issue more than any other, except for the Kingdom of God. Jesus said, "Watch out! Be on your guard against all kinds of greed; life does not consist in an abundance of possessions" (Luke 12:15 NIV).

Be on your guard: The challenge for us is to identify our 'needs' and to separate them from our unnecessary 'wants'. Finding that place where we are satisfied with where we are and what we have is a minefield in a busy and competitive world. A rich man was once asked 'How much is enough money?' He replied, 'Just a little bit more.'

Prayer:

Lord, help me to have a value system that is inspired by your life. Help me to treasure relationships more than possessions, and simplicity more than the clutter of materialism.

Amen.

The Stress Spider

"Wait for the Lord; be strong and take heart and wait for the Lord"

(Psalm 27:14 NIV).

If you had visited our house and scoured the rooms in search of spider webs you would not have been disappointed. I only became aware of our failure to dust well when a friend came to visit who had a slight phobia of spiders. Suddenly, I became very conscious that lurking high in crevices and corners of the rooms, we had accumulated a rather good collection of dusty and discarded examples. These had been building up for months and had gone unchecked. Some were even filled with the carcasses of left-over fly meals. Of course, it wasn't terrible, but given a few more months of neglect it could have been hired out to a horror film production company.

The real problem was not the webs, they are just a by-product of the problem. The issue was the spiders. If I could have found a way of eliminating those creepy crawlies, I wouldn't have dusty webs in the corners.

Spiderwebs are a good example of how we let stress build up and allow the by-product of continuing stress to affect our bodies, our relationship and ultimately, our walk with God. Gradually, we become entangled in a web of pressure that makes us feel like a walking carcass rather than a living soul. Many try to find a remedy in short term solutions. The hot tub industry sells the idea of relaxation for the mind, body and soul to take the stress away, but the warm waters only address the symptoms not the central problem or solution. The *'stress spider'* is still there waiting to spin a new web to entangle us.

Prayer:
Holy Spirit, in my times of stress help me discern the root causes rather than react to the manifestation of them. In my discomfort and fear, lead me to the place of peace. Give me wisdom to know what to let go of, both physically and mentally. Help me know security and peace in being a child of God.
Amen.

The Storm of Lockdown

Peace I leave with you; my peace I give you. I do not give to you as the world gives. Do not let your hearts be troubled and do not be afraid.

(John 14:27 NIV)

During the lockdowns, as the government brought in measures to control the spread of coronavirus, much of society was shut down. My own work in theatre stopped overnight. One day we were on a sell-out tour in Northern Ireland, the next day all theatre events were cancelled. I wandered around for days in a state of disbelief, trying to make sense of a world that had changed and my place in it seemed stolen. I had become a stranded refugee as time stood still. I was disorientated and stripped of my normality and security. My stability had been washed away by the growing pandemic. The sense of helplessness and fear sometimes brought unexpected bursts of tears as I mourned the loss of normality.

Throughout the country households barricaded themselves in units of isolation. Loved ones died alone, marriages were postponed, exams cancelled, and jobs lost. Our freedom was restricted by government, the rule book of social contact was rewritten. Shopping moved online, or we queued for our basic essentials in endless socially distanced lines.

It was hard to find peace in the sea of uncertainty and to plot a course when the compass seemed to have no true point of bearing, and when the harbour lights of safety seemed lost in the fog of the unknown. The battling wind and rolling waves of emotion took us from the crest of uncertainty to crushing despair. It was hard to find peace when it felt like you were drowning in a sea of despondency and depression. What use was it to hold on to the ship wheel when the rudder was broken? Where was hope when 'normal' had been washed overboard? With the daily swelling death toll how could we not be afraid? Society was so paralysed that we retreated and battened down the hatches to ride out the storm? Where was God's peace amongst it all?

In the harrowing gale of uncertainty, the words 'I am with you...do not be afraid. Peace I give unto you', are lost by the ferocious wind of circumstance. It was only when the storm subsided that we realised they *were* being spoken throughout that time ... it's just that we didn't hear.

Prayer

Peace perfect peace.
Lord at times the world seems a place of continuing fluctuating conflict and discord. The winds of disruption and personal suffering drown out your peace. At times I am over overwhelmed by the rising tides of turmoil in a world that seems often at war with itself. I see daily the news of yet more suffering and pain on my television.

Lord I pray for peace in a troubled world. I pray for world leaders to rise up and lead wisely and fairly. For leaders who will act beyond their own country's borders for the whole of humanity itself.

I pray for presidents, prime ministers and national leaders who hold the keys of change and fairness in their hands. I think of issues like Climate change, wars and food security. Lord, install in our leaders a righteousness and fairness. Guide them to bring peace to our troubled world.

Amen

The Titanic

"Greater love has no one than this: to lay down one's life for one's friends"

(John 15:13 NIV).

On the night of 14th/15th April 1912, *RMS Titanic* hit an iceberg and the resulting catastrophic damage gradually flooded the ship. When it became apparent that the Titanic – a ship considered unsinkable, was soon to be swallowed by the North Atlantic Ocean the order was given to load the lifeboats. However, at the time of construction, the original plans for thirty-two lifeboats were reduced to twenty, to stop the decks looking cluttered. Enough room for only for 1,178 of the estimated 2,200+ Passengers and crew. Captain Edward Smith ordered women and children to board the lifeboats first with just a few able men to row them away from the sinking ship.

It could have been total pandemonium with hordes of people scrabbling and fighting for the few places in the rafts. But the men acted in the spirit of love and courageously sacrificed their own lives for the sake of others. It was not the fittest or the wealthiest first, but women and children. The richest man on board that day and one of the wealthiest in the world was John Jacob Astor. He helped his pregnant young wife, her maid and nurse into a lifeboat then gave up his place to two scared children. The last reported sighting of him was smoking a cigarette half an hour before the vessel sunk. Reverend John Harper placed his sister and daughter into a life raft and went back to tell others about salvation. The Catholic priest Father Thomas Byles led first class passengers up the stairs to the lifeboats and helped women and children to board the life rafts. He then listened to confessions, recited the rosary and other prayers. Dozens of people huddled around him as they prayed and sung in their final moments. The seven-piece band continued to play on deck for over two hours to calm passengers. It is believed that their final piece was *Nearer My God to Thee*, shortly before the ship slipped beneath to a watery grave. Only twenty percent of men survived this great maritime tragedy. Among those who perished was Captain Smith who, as expected, went down with the vessel.

One hundred years later, the cruise vessel *Costa Concordia* ran aground in the Mediterranean off the coast near Tuscany with the loss of thirty-two lives. The captain himself abandoned the ship early, leaving many onboard to their own fate. The coastguard repeatedly ordered the captain to re-board the ship to help with the rescue, but he never did return. He was an example of every man for himself, a selfish act that may have contributed to the loss of lives.

Question: Would you have been one of the people who would have given up your place in a lifeboat for someone else?

The Wrong Coffee

"If your brother or sister sins, go and point out their fault, just between the two of you. If they listen to you, you have won them over"

(Matthew 18:15 NIV).

Conflict is never easy but complaining about another person is. When we feel upset or wronged, the easiest thing to do is start moaning to others about the person or situation rather than talking to the person involved themselves. In today's reading, we come across the biblical 'flow chart' of resolving interpersonal conflicts. First, let's identify some of the issues that cause conflict, either personal or in a group situation. Disagreements arise over people's differences, conflicting standards, actions, or a sense of ownership, or just a view or doctrine that is incompatible with your own. In the church you would think we would have perfected the art of good relationships, but we are far from it. We like to fall out over all kinds of things, from coffee blends to things central to our faith.

Here are a few examples of real scenarios that I have actually heard of. Some of them on the face of it seem improbable – almost unbelievable!

At a church, a disagreement broke out over Eucharist wine. A lady brought grape juice made from concentrated fruit instead of pure grapes for Sunday communion. This concentrated substitute was apparently wrong! It had to be pure grape juice that was served at communion. An ensuing argument broke out. *(Nothing like holy fellowship at the communion table - No mention of pure or concentrated grape juice in Matt. 26:26-28 NIV)*

Then, there was a church bust-up over the term 'potluck' instead of 'pot blessing'. (*Good luck in sorting that one out.*)

A couple of churches reported fights over the type of coffee to be served! One church was completely split about this and members left all because of the strength and blend of the coffee! *(Maybe they have now formed a new expression of church – The Right Blend Fellowship!).*

It has even been reported that church leaders have been known to have a punch up in the car park! *(Church leaders hit it off big time).*

These are all absurd examples, but sadly, they are all true. Unresolved disputes are a distraction from the mission of Jesus. It divides us rather than unites us. It makes us resentful rather than resourceful, bitter rather than blessed, and angry rather than cooperative. Matt. 18:15-17 (NIV) is our blueprint to relationship restoration. It tells us to approach and have a private conversation with the person we believe has wronged us, sharing our feelings, and challenging them that their actions may have been harmful. This gives them the opportunity to consider our viewpoint and hopefully work towards a positive outcome. The biblical principle is: get it sorted out quickly! Don't walk away!

Prayer:
Lord, I pray that in my relationships when disagreements arise that I will be bold in my attempts to bring restoration. I pray that I will be a good listener, and that even though I may feel angry, you will help me to stay calm. I pray that you give me strength and wisdom to make the first move, to sort the dispute. For your glory,
Amen.

Time to Move On

"After a long time had passed and the Lord had given Israel rest from all their enemies around them, Joshua, by then a very old man, summoned all Israel – their elders, leaders, judges and officials – and said to them: "I am very old. You yourselves have seen everything the Lord your God has done to all these nations for your sake; it was the Lord your God who fought for you"

(Joshua 23:1-3 NIV).

In politics, the time Prime Ministers spend in office nearly always ends in tears. They are either ousted by the electorate or their own party. The Iron Lady's, demise (Margaret Thatcher), came swiftly in her third term as Prime Minister. She had won three elections but eventually she became out of touch with events and the public.

Christian leaders who over the years have injected vision and energy into a ministry can also become tired and fatigued. When their passion becomes diminished they can get stuck in the groove of 'let's keep everything stable' – nothing too new, keep to the 'tried and tested'. The benefits of the 'tried and tested' method are that it can be a stable foundation and eliminate risk. The downside is that it can hold back innovation and prevent a true 'stepping out in faith', or any new expressions of praise to God.

Life is a revolving door of generations coming and going. In leadership, whether you're the occupant of 10 Downing Street or the top dog at church, there will be a time to step down. No leader should outstay their calling and block God's plan for the next generation of ground-breakers. Current leaders have a responsibility to ensure that the succession of leadership continues beyond their time; to prepare them for good work and instil in them the foundation of godly principles.

If you continue to read the whole chapter of Joshua 23, you will see that Joshua knew his time of leadership had come to an end. This passage is Joshua's retirement speech, cementing his legacy and instructing the next generation to stay within God's will. He laid a strong foundation for those who followed.

The next generation of trailblazers may introduce new expressions of worship, revamp the children's ministry, and reach out to the community in innovative ways. This is something to celebrate. There is no greater legacy for a retired leader, than the person who follows you achieving even greater things than yourself. That way, it won't end in tears of sadness but shouts of joy.

Trenches and Razor Wire

"A gentle answer turns away wrath, but a harsh word stirs up anger"

(Proverbs 15.1 NIV).

Overcoming a disagreement and working through an issue can deepen a relationship. I would say that deep friends are made out of good times shared and difficulties overcome together. But sadly, human nature has a habit of digging a trench and putting up the razor wire of self-defence, firing back rather than looking for peace. Proud people rarely give ground and can be too quick to draw up the battle lines.

This verse gives us guidance on how to defuse a situation and encourages us to stop looking for the knockout punch to win the argument. The problem with trying to land a knockout punch is that it usually misses, and the other person starts throwing counter punches. Aggression never wins an argument.

There is another way: 'A gentle answer turns away wrath, but a harsh word stirs up anger.'

The motivating factor behind resolving conflict is to bring restoration to the relationship, rather than walk away head held high in victory. Give grace to the adversary.

Understanding Conflict in the Body of Christ

One time or another, everyone has been wronged by another person. Maybe we've been lied to, mistreated, made fun of or stolen from. There are people who use aggressive language to enforce their point, attacking the character of others or undermining their position through sarcasm. Others are skilled at manipulation and use it for their own personal gain at the expense of others.

Since childhood we have developed ways of dealing with conflict, either by trial or error, or by observation. Some of us will think, 'surely, it's better to avoid the problem, turn the other cheek, just forget that the conflict ever happened – forgive and forget ... right?' The denial approach is one of 'anything for a quiet life'. But this reaction never leads to a balanced relationship. There will always be mistrust and suspicion.

When it comes to our brothers and sisters in Christ, the Bible gives us very specific instructions on how to deal with conflict.

"If your brother or sister sins, go and point out their fault, just between the two of you. If they listen to you, you have won them over. But if they will not listen, take one or two others along, so that 'every matter may be established by the testimony of two or three witnesses.' If they still refuse to listen, tell it to the church; and if they refuse to listen even to the church, treat them as you would a pagan or a tax collector"

(Matthew 18: 15-17 NIV).

This verse provides a route map for dealing with confrontation in the body of Christ. It doesn't say, roll over and put up with unrighteous actions or words. It's does say: Do something, take action, get help to bring understanding. This verse is a vehicle to bring balance, restore relationship and resolution in situations of conflict. It is about healing rather that victory.

Prayer:

Holy Spirit, I pray that the way I handle conflict will bring peace and not discord. That it will bring harmony rather than tension. Bring resolution rather than confusion.
I pray for the skills of listening more than persuasive words. I pray for humility rather than a proud posturing position. I pray for understanding rather than victory. I pray that I will reflect God's goodness, and show his forgiveness.

Amen

Unusual Song Studio

"I am in the midst of lions; I am forced to dwell among ravenous beasts – men whose teeth are spears and arrows, whose tongues are sharp swords"

(Psalm 57:4 NIV).

There are some unusual places to write a poetic song, and hiding in a cave is certainly one of them. The best lyrics are often written out of personal experience and tell a story. The background to Psalm 57 written by David, was that he was on the run from King Saul.

After a couple of instances where the king had used him as target practise for spear throwing, David had decided that Saul was losing the plot. It had become clear to him that it would be better to be a fugitive than a dead harp player. So, David was driven into exile and soon became public enemy number one. He initially escaped to Gath, and then moved on and found himself a 'back to basics' cave at Adullam, a location on the margins of both Saul's kingdom and the enemy Philistine territory. David was in a desperate place, not just emotionally and physically, but in terms of its location. They say when choosing a dwelling it's all about 'location, location, location.' Unfortunately, this new cave encampment would not be marketable by any estate agent. Situated on the borders of warring kingdoms, it was not a place of comfort or good amenities, but one of desperation and distress.

In this psalm, David expresses his distress to God; a cathartic moment where the inward volcano of anguish erupts to the surface in a lava of words that show deep lament. However, on the positive side, it was also a place where he found God's protection.

It is better to be in a cave under God's protection than in a palace outside the will of God.

Victory Turns Sour

The Philistines had defeated the Israelites. Imagine the Philistine's victory parade, crowds lining the streets, watching their army troop past. Imagine hearing the crowd cheering wildly. To top it all, they had captured the Ark of the Covenant, the very box that contained the Israelites' most powerful Godly relic. They rejoiced that they had weakened their enemy both physically and spiritually. But their jubilation soon turned sour when something odd began to happen. A chain of mysterious, strange and alarming occurrences made them feel like they were living in a horror movie.

The Philistines had placed the Ark in their dragon's temple. The next morning, they discovered that one of the dragon statues had crashed face down in front of the Ark. After standing the statue up again, the next morning they discovered it had once again fallen in front of the Ark and smashed. Things only got worse, people of the city developed tumours. They concluded that it was related to the Ark of the Covenant, which was somehow cursing them. So they moved it on to Gath, which went down like a lead balloon with the people there who were already suffering. Then they tried to off-load it to the City of Ekron but its reputation proceeded its arrival and the Ekronians threw an almighty wobbly. This was one hot potato they didn't want. The Philistine leadership gathered and decided to return the Ark of the Covenant to its rightful owners and rid themselves of all the infection it was causing. So, they drew up plans to return the dangerous object to the Israelites.

There are some important lessons we can learn from this. What the Philistines unlawfully acquired turned out to be a curse for them. It reminded me of a friend who, while on holiday took a liking to the rocks on a beach and thought he would make a nice rockery in his garden. So secretly after several trips up and down the coastal steps, he collected several sacks full of rocks and transported them home to build a new garden feature. Nothing untoward happened, the kitchen cupboards didn't suddenly open in the middle of the night and the crockery didn't crash to the floor, the microwave didn't blow up or the washing machine didn't catch fire and no one developed cancer in the family.

All was well until he tried to sell his house. It was priced fairly, they had viewings, but while similar houses on the housing market were being snapped up no one wanted to buy his home. This continued for a considerable amount of time. He pondered why, then remembered the stones he'd taken from the beach. They weren't his, his garden wasn't the place for them. So convicted by the Holy Spirit, he made another trip to the beach, this time lugging the heavy stones down the coastal path to their rightful home ... you can guess the end of the story, straightaway the house sold!

You could argue that all this was just coincidence, but I believe there are spiritual principles in this Bible passage. We shouldn't ever take what isn't ours. There is a spiritual cost to all our actions.

(Suggested reading: 1 Samuel Chapters 4-6 NIV)

What the Farmyard Taught Me about Walking Circumspectly

"See then that ye walk circumspectly, not as fools, but as wise, redeeming the time, because the days are evil,"

(Ephesians 5:15-16 KJV).

As a kid, I loved to stomp around my uncle's dairy farm in deepest Somerset, especially to help him herd the cows into the yard at milking time. My mum insisted I pull on my wellies because, well... you know, cows have a habit of creating a minefield that can only be navigated by experts in solving mazes. I remember carefully tiptoeing across the yard, plotting a zigzag path to the milking shed, determined not to get my sparkly wellies dirty. You could say that I 'walked circumspectly' – that is, carefully avoiding the potential catastrophe of falling face-first into a steaming cow-pie.

This world is full of 'cow-pies'. Through my half-century of life, I've discovered the best way to avoid landing in the proverbial pile of fresh manure is to heed the Bible's advice: to watch intently where I'm walking, not to be foolish ... and to make wise use of the time God has given me. My time left here is shorter today than it was yesterday – and so is yours.

Our world, if you hadn't noticed, is deteriorating rapidly; physically, but far more seriously, morally. Signs are all around us. We don't have long to go before the climactic day the Bible talks about – when Jesus will return to this earth to put things right.

I don't want to be face down in the manure pile when that day arrives. I want to be on my feet – walking carefully and deliberately with God in faith, love, holiness, and purity, avoiding the cow pies.

How about you? Are you walking circumspectly?

Julian Lukins

What is Dying ?

What is dying?
I am standing on the seashore.
A ship sails to the morning breeze and starts for the ocean.
She is an object of beauty and I stand watching her
Till at last she fades from the horizon,
And someone at my side says "She is gone!" Gone! Where?
Gone from my sight, that is all;
She is just as large in the masts, hull and spars
as she was when I saw her,
And just as able to bear her load of living freight to its destination.
The diminished size and total loss of sight is in me, not in her;
And just at the moment when someone at my side says, "She is gone",
There are others who are watching her coming,
And other voices take up a glad shout,
'There she comes'– and that is dying. 3.

3. Ref: Brent, Bishop , Charles ,Henry. *(1862- 1929). The Sailing Ship*

Who Am I ?

Have you ever asked yourself, 'Who am I?' Could you summarize your identity into a short phrase? Maybe you would use something like the following:

'I am a Mother' or, 'I am 'Wife'.
'I am a Father' or, 'I am a 'Husband'.

Maybe you'd use a job to describe your identity:

'I am a Managing Director'.
'I am a Gardener'.
'I am a Doctor'.
'I am a Plumber'.
'I am a Nurse'.
'I am a Social Worker'.
'I am a Widow'.

When professional theatre actors take on a role, they embrace their character's manner, their reactions, posture and even voice in order for the production to be authentic. It is as though the actor puts on another skin, masking out every trait of their own persona and immersing themselves to become an entirely different person. When live on stage, they aim to convince the audience that the person they are watching is real, emotionally drawing them into the highs and lows of that character's journey for a couple of hours. The actor loses himself inside the person he is playing.

At the end of the play, and after an exhausting run of back-to-back shows, it has been known for actors who have been totally immersed in the role, to walk out of the backstage door and totally forget their own name, the number of the bus home, and even be confused about where they live! To help with mental health and give actors a 'touch base moment', some theatres have introduced an exercise to bring them back to reality. The exercise comprises the show's cast sitting in a circle and in turn they hold a mirror and stare directly into it. Then someone asks them the following questions, which they have to reply to as they continue to stare in the mirror.

217

Question:	What is your name?
Answer: -	*I am (real name)*
Question: -	What is your date of birth?
A*nswer: -*	*My date of birth is (real date of birth)*
Question:	What is your father's name?
Answer: -	*My father's name is (real name)*
Question:	What is your phone number?
Answer: -	*My phone number is (real number)*
Question:	What is your favorite sport?
Answer:	*My favorite sport is ......*

The aim of the exercise is to bring them back to reality and to remember Who they are.

If you are someone who proclaims to have a living faith, I challenge you; how would you answer the summary questions about who you are? Would you first say you were a parent, state your profession – your interests? Maybe you would think about deeper things, like telling us that you are a creative person ... or even a religious one!

But who are you primarily?

I believe that primarily we are simply 'a disciple of Jesus'.

William Tyndale
The First English Bible

In the time of Henry VIII, England was a place of spiritual darkness for the common man who had no personal Bible. The Roman Catholic church had control of how the written word of God was communicated. This was through priests who often mumbled through services in Latin, which few could understood. At that time the church was corrupt from the head down, even the Pope had illegitimate children. No message of personal salvation was heard from the pulpit.

William Tyndale was a bright young Cambridge scholar who was frustrated that the common man had no direct access to the Word of God. He wanted to rectify this by translating the scriptures and producing an English Bible, thus enabling every household the opportunity to read the word of God for themselves. However, to produce an English translation of scripture he would need permission through the proper channels. His plans drew dismay from the clergy and from Rome and the door was firmly shut. Against the wishes of Rome and at the risk of persecution and even death, he was determined to progress. At that time, England was not a safe place to attempt a translation from Greek and Hebrew to English. Even if he succeeded with the text, the chances were that no printer would dare to attempt the printing of his translation anyway. So, he slipped away to the continent without the king's consent and began his painstaking work there living anonymously in Europe while trying to avoid the king's agents who were in pursuit.

After completing his New Testament in the English language, he started the printing process. However, his activities were discovered, and he had to flee. Tyndale escaped to Worms, Germany. There he printed the first editions of the New Testament without hindrance. In 1526 trading ships bound for London, carried the first translations, hidden in bales of cotton and sacks of flour. For the first time, a printed English version of the New Testament became available for the price of one shilling.

The king issued a decree that the books should be burnt if found. It became a serious offence to buy and even handle one of the books. A person would be excommunicated or charged with heresy and thrown into prison. Hundreds of books were intercepted. At one stage, to stem the flow of Tyndale translation, the authorities devised a scheme to buy up all the books which made everyone happy. Merchants had their money; the bishops oversaw the burning of the books and Tyndale had money to fund his next edition.

Tyndale moved to Antwerp for better smuggling routes to England but this came with the increased risk of being captured. For nine years he managed to evade authorities, but a man called Henry Phillips gained Tyndale's confidence and hatched a plan to kidnap him and deliver him to the king. Phillips lured Tyndale directly to waiting soldiers. Tyndale was captured and then imprisoned for eighteen months. He was tried and condemned as a heretic. He was executed by strangulation and then burned at the stake.

After Tyndale's death and Henry VIII's fall out with the Pope over his marriage to Catherine of Aragon, the king allowed the bible to be printed in England. In 1538 the king ordered every parish to purchase a copy for public display. All the new Bibles were based on Tyndale's work but did not carry his name.

Xenodocheionology

Xenodocheionology, means the study of hotels and inns. Here we are going to explore travel and the Inns and hotels of biblical times. Firstly, we must dispel our twenty-first century image of Premium Inns, Travel Lodges or a Super 8 Motel, where you book online and arrive in a room to find a bed made with sheets, a TV and coffee and tea-making facilities. We must also view travel as a means to get from one place to another rather than a pleasure.

In both the Old and New Testament, traveling around the orient was only done when it was a necessity. In Old Testament times preparing for any sort of trip was a huge palaver. Before a person set off he had to 'pay all debts, provide for dependents, give parting gifts, return all articles under trust and organise food and water.

The journeys were measured in units of days (Genesis 30.36 NIV) rather than distance and were uncomfortable affairs, fraught with danger from bandits and wild animals. For security, men often travelled in large groups, occasionally on foot but usually on the backs of horses, mules, or donkeys. For desert routes camels were mostly used. To escape both the intense heat and detection from robbers, caravans of people would travel at night, often with the help of a guide who would navigate by the stars finding various watering holes and resting places. Psalm 107 tells a story when a journey didn't go quite to plan, until God answered their prayers.

"Some wandered in desert wastelands,
finding no way to a city where they could settle.
They were hungry and thirsty,
and their lives ebbed away.
Then they cried out to the Lord in their trouble,
and he delivered them from their distress.
He led them by a straight way
to a city where they could settle."

(Psalm 107: 4-7 NIV)

The 'Inns' of Old Testament days were merely stopping places for travellers overnight comprising of a tent or perhaps a cave. An extreme wild camping experience.

In Jesus' time it was a religious duty to give hospitality which could mean, being entertained at a Bedouin tent encampment or a village guest room or a guest chamber or room in a private home. The story of Mary and Joseph's accommodation woes are recorded in the Gospel of St. Luke 2:7 (NIV) "There was no room for them in the inn".

From childhood we are fed a common narrative picturing Joseph after hours of travelling, in desperation banging on door of the local bed and breakfast, to find a place where Mary can give birth to Jesus. Then the rude innkeeper slams the door closed in his face with the words 'no room'. It is believed that 'The Inn' in this story was not a commercial enterprise but a house with a guest room. The Greek word for 'Inn' included in this story (Kataluma), means guest room not the modern 'Inn' as translated in English.

Luke's gospel tells the story of the 'Good Samaritan', (Luke 10:34,35 NIV). This gives us an insight into both the continuing risks of traveling and the mention of an 'Inn' with an Inn keeper. In Roman and Greek times 'Inns' existed. The Greek word used in the above passage is 'Pandocheion', meaning public house for the reception of strangers. This maybe the nearest the New Testament gets to a travel lodge or fully inclusive hotel.

Your Pain

"He will wipe every tear from their eyes. There will be no more death or mourning or crying or pain, for the old order of things has passed away"

(Revelation 21:4 NIV).

I am having a rather bad day because I am experiencing toothache The pain has been fairly constant and there are moments of acute sharpness that are so intense that I am unable to speak. But for all my agony I am aware that this pain is nothing compared to what others suffer on a daily basis.

So, what does pain teach us?

It teaches us we are vulnerable, we are not Robinson Crusoe, completely isolated trying to survive by ourselves. The effects of pain push us to seek help from others.

A few years ago, I became very poorly on a trip to West Africa and was taken to a very basic hospital. The doctor prescribed medication, but it was the family's responsibility to care for the practical needs of the patient. Being over 1,000 miles away this was a problem, especially as I didn't have the strength to support my own weight or wash myself. Fortunately, a young Dutch backpacker took pity on me. Twice a day, she would get me out of bed, help me to the washroom, undress and wash me. Was I embarrassed? No, because I was in a desperate situation and needed practical intervention. She was an angel in my time of need.

Pain and illness can be totally debilitating and isolating and yet pain gives opportunities for others to intervene, to assist, to care, to minister.

Pain is a vehicle that teaches:

The Hurt – how to receive

The Carer – how to administer.

Pain is never easy to deal with, and as our bodies age, it may become a regular unwelcome visitor. The great news is that one day God promises pain will be no more. He will wipe every tear from suffering eyes. There will be no more death, mourning or crying, for the old order of things has will have passed away.

Youth with a Mission - The Loren Cunningham Story

The founder of Youth with a Mission (YWAM) came from a family of traveling evangelists. At thirteen he delivered his first sermon about temptation. In his book *Is that really you God?* He recalls how, when he was knelt praying one time, he could see the words of Mark 16:15-16 (NIV) before him: 'Go ye into all the world and preach the gospel to every creature'. Another vision came to him – 'wave upon wave of young people in their teens and twenties, marching onto the shores of all the continents of the world'. God's role in Loren's life was huge: He was only twenty and there were plenty of generous employment offers, but he turned them down as he felt God was calling him elsewhere. After bible college, he organized his first missionary trip with 105 young people to Hawaii. It was only a partial success, half of the team wanted to relax on the beaches while the others shared their faith. He learnt that the volunteers needed a single focus for the mission. Personally however, he felt incomplete, he lacked a personal soulmate. He constantly wondered, where would he find a girl who would engage with his vision of recruiting young volunteers for God?

In December 1960 he founded, *Youth with a Mission.* Loren's bedroom became an office, then the expansion into the garage took place. Equipped with a typewriter and a mimeograph machine they produced their plans to lead a Christian service for which none of them received any renumeration. On missions to share the Christian message there would be rugged evangelism and no dating! The reaction was mixed; the young people were excited, but church leaders were unenthusiastic as they feared these ill-trained young people descending upon their mission fields and damaging established missionary work.

It was suggested that if his volunteers were sent out to existing compounds and supervised, he may be onto a winner. Liberia was the first opportunity for the first set of YWAM volunteers. Two bulldozer drivers helped build a road to an area that was known to be home to several lepers. A continuing trickle of recruits came, but this didn't amount to the wave of young people he had envisioned.

Two years later, while visiting friends, he met his future wife, Darlene. After their honeymoon weekend they set out on a mission trip through Europe and Asia. This was followed by organising twenty-four small teams to go to the Dominican Republic. Two churches were started as a result.

Despite all his hard work, disappointment came from his own denomination. They wanted him to carry on with his vision, but with a more manageable number of volunteers. He was a drummer out of beat with the band, so he gave up his paid position and stepped out in faith.

Six years had now passed since YWAM's creation, more workers became full-time, and the volunteer workforce grew to a few hundred. This was still not an acceptable level to Loren however. After five years of marriage Loren and Darlene started a family.

In the autumn of 1967, bedridden with flu, a word came to Loren that they were to start a school to disciple students in the ways of God – it would be both classroom-based and involve practical travel missions to many foreign lands. They would share the good news about Jesus and help others. There were set backs with many of their starting ventures falling through. They eventually found an old derelict hotel with thirty-two rooms. Here they were able to set-up a solid base. This was to be the first school which eventually it took in thirty-six students.

The course became a springboard for many of the young people and yielded new ministries under the umbrella of YWAM. The number of worldwide staff crept up to forty. Another turning point came with one thousand young people going to evangelise at the Munich Olympic games. Miraculously, a castle was bought to house some young people and this then became a permanent German base. The organization grew some more, and the vision of thousands of young volunteers became a reality, with workers being sent to over sixty countries and the acquisition of thirty-five bases around the world.

The Cunningham's next adventure was to take them to Hawaii. After three years, and moving home eighteen times, a fifty-five-acre farm was given to them and converted into a discipleship training school. The YWAM university followed in a formerly derelict hotel. The university saw a fresh wave of evangelism as thousands of young minds moulded by Christ entered society to communicate God's grace to others. Then followed the Anastasia ship, a perfect tool for both mercy and evangelical ministries.

Loren's vision had materialised. Today, thousands have undertaken and completed short-term missions and attended YWAM training schools; but, more importantly, many have started their own ministries as a direct result of their time in YWAM. The organisation is now working in 180 countries. There have been waves of young people touching thousands of lives.

Footnote:

Suddenly, unannounced, Loren Cunningham appeared on the island of Guernsey to visit the YWAM team I was jointly heading up. He was on a tour to visit every country of the world. The moment seemed fleeting, and I never quite took on board that I had met the founder of Youth with a Mission. But I remember what he said to me, 'We must pray for the nations.' I was one of thousands of young people who responded to God's call to join the organization he founded. I learnt valuable lessons which helped me start a ministry in theatre arts, which has performed to thousands. Many others have done similar work spreading the good news. The good thing about this story is it became more about an organization that would 'Know God and make Him known'. 4.

4. Ref: Cunningham, L. and Rogers, J., 2001. *Is That Really You, God?*.

Zacchaeus

"For the Son of Man came to seek and save what was lost"

(Luke 19:10 NIV).

We come to the last story in this series of devotions and what better conclusion than to visit the key message of Jesus and to see how meeting Jesus transforms a life. This is told through the story of Zacchaeus.

Zacchaeus, based in the region of Jericho was a tax collector for the Roman empire at the time of Jesus; a position that gave him a rather lucrative pay packet. However, the flip side of this was he was despised by his own Jewish community for working for the enemy. Zacchaeus was a descendant of Abraham, a Jew in name but not in practice. He was a man who had betrayed his national identity for personal wealth. And as if that wasn't enough, he had alienated his community further by manipulating the system, lining his pockets by extracting additional tax from his countrymen. Zacchaeus was recorded as being short, but he was not 'short of a few bob in the bank' due to his scheming. Ironically, the Hebrew meaning of his name means 'pure,innocent'... which he was far from.

When Jesus rocks into town, Zacchaeus is determined not to miss the action. Taking a vantage point up a tree he can then clearly see all the commotion the crowd are making. Then, Jesus eyeballs Zacchaeus balancing on the branches and to Zacchaeus' shock, Jesus then invites himself and his motley crew too his home. Suddenly 'Zac the Tax' is propelled from a position of observer to that of central character and the host to Jesus and his entourage. This sends the community into a heightened state of gossip. Is Jesus going to visit a sinner?

Zac was undone by Jesus' presence. It was as if all his past wrong actions and words had, metaphorically come rolling down a hill knocking him for six. Convinced of his sin, Zacchaeus instantaneously offered restitution to those he had wronged. This was the fruit of his repentance in action, a change of direction. Jesus who had come to seek and to save the lost had transformed another life.

What do we learn from this story?

Meeting Jesus can reveal to us, what we didn't always know about ourselves - uncovering our hidden sin. Responding to Jesus' message of repentance takes us from a place of disconnection with God to a fully connective relationship with God the father.

Prayer:

Lord I want to know the power of your presence in my life. The filling of your Holy spirit daily reveals your ways. Use me Lord as a light in the darkness, a beacon of hope in people's despair. May I be a conduit of love and kindness. May my actions and words bring healing. May the fruit of my repentance enable me to walk humbly in truth and free me from my past mistakes. For the glory of God, the son and the holy spirit

Amen.

ABOUT THE AUTHOR

BARRY BOYTON is the founder of Oddments Theatre Company and has a diploma in theatre arts. He is an author and script writer of both sketches and plays which have been seen by thousands of people. He is known for producing work that tells a strong story and creates a visual memory. His passion is to share the Christian message in a thought-provoking and amusing way. He tours regularly with major shows such as *The Hiding Place*, *Amazing Grace* and *The Road to the Cross,* performing in churches and prisons. This is Barry's second book. the first one being a story-telling theatre sketch book entitled *Fish and Chips*.

Barry is married to Marion, and they have two daughters. He also has a keen interest in politics and is a councillor for the town of Yeovil in Somerset, England.

REFERENCES

Bible references: All Bible references are followed by the appropriate abbreviation: NIV- New International Version, KJV- King James Version, GNT: Good News Translation, MSG – The Message: Eugene H. Peterson.

1. Ref: Magnusson, Sally, 1981, *The Flying Scotsman,* Published by Quarter Books

2. Ref: Nettleton, Asahel, Quote, *Azquotes.com.* Description, *Wikipedia*

3. Ref: Brent, Bishop, Charles, Henry *(1862-1929), The Sailing Ship*

4. Ref: Cunningham, L. and Rogers, J., 2001, *Is That Really You, God?* YWAM Publishing, 2nd ed. Seattle, Wa, p.8.